PLAYING THE GAME
Life after Sports

Benjamin J. Gilmore

Copyright 2023 © Benjamin J. Gilmore

All rights reserved.

No part of this book may be reproduced, stored in a retrieval system, or transmitted by any means, electronic, mechanical, photocopying, recording, or otherwise, without written permission from the author.

ISBN (Paperback): 979-8-9882956-9-3
ISBN (eBook): 979-8-9882956-8-6

Table of Contents

Is Life Just a Game?..1

Where We Are 15

Clarity..21

FEAR..33

Coachability...51

Financial Freedom...59

Self-Denial..71

Competition, Comparison, and Common Sense..............93

Happiness..101

Our Relationship with God 115

CHAPTER 1

Is Life Just a Game?

The Beginning of the End

Championship game, full count, top of the 7th, 2 outs, runner on 2nd, down by 1 run and I was in the batter's box. This was the moment I was made for. I'd fantasized about this a million times before. The only differences: the fantasy was Game 7 of the World Series, bottom of the ninth, bases loaded.

In summer of 2006, I batted 3rd in the lineup for the Doniphan County American Legion baseball team. We'd had a better-than-expected season, based on preseason predictions. We were young, but we had some great talent and gritty competitors. My last campaign with Post 155 was shaping up to be a Cinderella story.

Playing the Game

We were playing for the Zone Championship with a State Championships berth on the line. Our competitor was Seneca/Nemaha County, a team we had beaten earlier in the season but a very solid club with serious talent. They wore green and yellow jerseys with the old-school yellow baseball sock stirrups reminiscent of a team from the 1970s. Mustaches and sideburns weren't popular in 2006, though.

I'd faced this pitcher before. I knew his tendencies, and I had his speed timed. I was confident.

The first pitch was a slider that seemed to cross outside but was a called strike. Next was a fastball that missed inside. Third pitch was a high fastball above the zone, and fourth was a curveball that hit the dirt.

3–1. Here comes the meatball.

Fastball on the outside corner. I went with the pitch and swung hard and level.

"Foul!"

Five feet outside the first base line in right field.

3–2. Here comes the curve.

I moved up 8 inches from my usual spot in the box and inched a little closer to the plate. I knew what was coming. All I had to do was drive it to the outfield to tie the game.

But…

A homer puts us up 1.

The pitcher gave his usual curveball que and starts his windup.

Delivers the pitch.

The ball is coming right down the middle.

It's hanging.

I swing with everything I've got.

Whiff!

"Strike three! Ballgame!"

This must be a bad dream.

I misjudged the timing of the break and tried to pull it for a home run. Was it pride? Was it arrogance? Did I underestimate my opponent? If I had focused and driven the ball instead of pulling my head, I would have given my team a shot to complete the comeback.

My baseball career was over. And my last at bat was a strikeout. This couldn't be real.

• • •

Falling in Love

Growing up in rural Kansas was truly a blessing. Many might think living in a town of 1,000 people sounds less than appealing, but for me, at least, it was heaven. Yes, everyone truly knows everyone, and word travels faster than the speed of light. But when someone needs help, it's amazing to see the community come together to lend a helping hand.

Living in a tight-knit community meant I couldn't get away with *anything*, and believe me, if I ever stepped out of line, my parents knew about it before they got home. But it also meant our town was safe enough for my brother and I to roam with our buddies all summer. We spent most of our time just across the street from my grandparents' house at the grade school playing football, baseball, and basketball. We'd usually have six to ten neighborhood kids to play with, which was perfect for just about any game we wanted to play.

Summertime meant baseball games twice a week. My dad was my baseball and basketball coach until seventh grade, and he instilled a competitive spirit in me at an early age. He taught me the importance of focus and visualizing success. "See yourself making great plays," he would say. "The more you practice, the more prepared for success you'll be." Over and over, he would repeat this ritualistic rhetoric until I was finishing his sentences. He was my biggest critic and my biggest fan. I lived and died on his opinion.

I started playing organized baseball in first grade, but those first couple of years were about learning the fundamentals. I enjoyed playing, but I wanted to be just like the "big kids" who were pitching and stealing bases.

Do you remember the first time you fell in love? I have a vivid memory of my moment. I was eight years old, and it was a perfect summer night on the diamond under the lights, the smell of nachos and popcorn blending with the freshly cut grass. We were ahead by one run at the bottom of the final inning. We had two outs, and the opposing team had a solid hitter at the plate. I knew beyond a shadow of a doubt that he was going to hit me a ground ball at shortstop, and I was throwing him out to win the game. I told myself over and over again, *He's hitting it to me, I'm making this play, and we're going to win the game.* On the first pitch, that exact scenario played out. I was hooked. I didn't realize it at the time, but baseball had become the gateway to my sports love affair.

Winning was expected, and losing was unacceptable, even in the early years. But that was the point, right? Winning was fun, and losing sucked. It wasn't like so many of the youth leagues now where every kid gets a participation trophy. Maybe part of it was the cost to buy all the medals (the league I played in didn't have a lot of money in the early 1990s), but if you didn't get 1st, 2nd, or 3rd, you didn't get squat. I loved it. The thrill of besting the competition and the pride of accomplishing a goal with your teammates were exhilarating, not to mention getting some unique hardware.

Dad was a master at balancing high expectations and supportive reinforcement. I remember one year Dad had a conversation with the team at the end of the season before the final tournament.

"Boys," his serious facial expression and tone commanded everyone's unflinching attention.

"We can play this tournament just like we played the regular season, where everybody gets to play, regardless of the score. Or we can go for a *gold* medal. Not everyone will get playing time, but everyone would get a *gold* medal if we win. What do you want to do?"

Our team of third and fourth graders unanimously approved the latter option to go for gold, some fully knowing they wouldn't set foot on the field. I bet you can guess what happened. I remember the team's excitement when we were crowned champions. The looks on everyone's faces, even those that didn't get to play, were priceless. We were *all* gold medalists.

But the feeling quickly faded. After the short ceremony and a few photos, some parents started badgering Dad and the other coaches about not playing their kids. In their minds, every kid should have been able to play in the championship game even though it was a close, hard-fought win. Dad explained the options he gave us before the tournament and that everyone was given the opportunity to have a say. He also pointed out the looks on their sons' faces after getting their gold medal. It didn't make the parents any more pleased, but it closed the argument, and it taught me two valuable lessons:

1. Winning (success) and playing time require sacrifice by means of practice and hard work.
2. I would *never* be ok with losing or riding the bench.

•••

The Bottom

"I'm done."

As I sat in his small, windowless office for our post-season review, I told my receivers coach I was quitting the football team.

For the last two years, I had committed what seemed like my entire waking hours to an even split of football and schoolwork at a small, private college. In my mind, I was better than a few of the guys dressing for games, but my efforts to secure that sacred gameday jersey seemed to be in vain—a stark contrast from high school where I was a varsity starter from my sophomore year on. A sport I once loved had become a glaringly hollow obligation. It was December 2007, and my grades were abysmal, I was failing at relationships with people I loved, and I was emotionally drained. The answer seemed clear: quitting football would allow me to focus on school, work, family, and friends, which would serve me best in the future.

I wouldn't be making a living playing football, and since I didn't have a scholarship, my time would be better served earning money and improving my GPA. The logic seemed sound, but I had no idea of the profound psychological impact to come... or what had been coming for a long time and just hadn't manifested yet.

I had spent my entire life not just playing sports, but sports *were* my life. My purpose in life, my *identity*, and my sense of worth were directly associated with a progressive compilation of athletic accomplishments. Now, that purpose was gone.

Three months had passed since I quit football.

The dark, bitter cold of winter was serving as a catalyst for the toxic mixture of depression, anxiety, doubt, guilt, and shame. My white-walled coffin of a room was as sterile as my worthless life. I was in an inescapable hole of misery without any hope of salvation. I had let down everyone that meant something to me, people that believed in me and who supported me for so many years through so many different sports. Most of all, I was letting down my dad. I wanted him to be proud of me more than anything. The proudest I'd ever seen him was when I accomplished something great on the field. The most disappointed I'd ever seen him was when I messed up bad on the field.

I wanted to end my life.

I opened the bathroom medicine cabinet and stared at the giant bottle of ibuprofen. I could just swallow it all, and then I wouldn't have to suffer anymore.

But something stopped me: I could suddenly see the real impact this decision would have on my parents, my brother, my sister, my girlfriend, my grandparents, and my friends. I didn't think I was worth saving, and I certainly didn't think I was loveable, but this decision wouldn't just make them sad for a while. I realized that killing myself would ruin the lives of the people I loved most. Was it worth it to take them down with me? Even at my lowest, my love for them completely outweighed my self-hatred. But although I loved them and I knew they loved me, I still felt completely alone.

Nobody knew, because in my mind, I held onto the false theory that showing any weakness ruins your reputation forever. At my lowest, I'm sure it was evident that I wasn't happy, and something was amiss, but even when I wasn't suicidal, the depression and anxiety kept me in a cloud of confusion and self-doubt. My apathy for accomplishing anything was barely concealed by the mask I wore every day. I was a pro at doing just enough to get by without raising suspicion.

To be honest, depression had been stealing pieces of my life since eighth grade. I couldn't admit that I felt worthless because tough guys don't talk about feelings. We put our head down and get the job done. No complaining. No excuses. So, I hid behind comedy, charisma, and false-confidence — all masks.

Choosing life didn't make me happy. In fact, I continued to silently struggle with depression and suicidal thoughts throughout the remainder of college. As my athletic career disintegrated, I had a thought that would plague me for years to come:

Life is just a game.

A rigged game in which only people with a special connection, or special talent, or special intelligence, or special you-fill-in-the-blank succeed. And I wasn't special anymore.

To be successful at this game, you had to get a great job, make a lot of money, wear the right clothes, have a lot of friends, possess a confidence that borders on arrogance, and follow all the other societal rules that we worship so dutifully.

Life was just like sports. The only question that needed to be answered was, "Who is the best?" And just like Ricky Bobby said in *Talladega Nights*, "If you ain't first, yer last."

No matter how successful you become, there's always someone better. So what's the point?

Fast-forward to today.

I'm very happily married to my high school sweetheart, and we have three absolutely beautiful little girls. I consider myself to be a happy person who has a clear vision of where I want my life to go. I have a fulfilling career that challenges me and offers me the opportunity to truly help people. I have served as a volunteer on several councils, boards, and committees. I'm not someone that will tell you they don't have any regrets because I have *plenty*. But I will tell you that I look at my mistakes as lessons, and I've learned to forgive myself and commit to being a better person.

So, what changed? How did I go from having suicidal thoughts and barely able to function to being hungry for life and ready for the curveballs?

I decided to **try**.

Try something new, a different approach. (Spoiler alert: it ended up being something that had been with me since I was a child.)

For anyone that's dealt with chronic depression and anxiety, you know the feelings of desperation and hopelessness. It doesn't just steal your joy; it also forces you into a pit and spoon-feeds you an endless supply of fear. But when I realized that my hands weren't tied, I also realized that I could choose to search for a way out of the pit. Since suicide was off the table, my only choice was to get better.

I was able to move forward by the grace of God and strengthening my relationship with my Lord and Savior Jesus Christ. I poured myself into personal development books and programs that focused on the areas of life that we will discuss in this book. I don't take antidepressants or other drugs, but that's not reality for everyone. If you're struggling right now, please, please, please know these:

1. *You* are loved.
2. There's no sin so big God can't forgive.
3. Pray. There's no right way. Just ask God into your heart.
4. Seek help. It's not being weak. It's actually one of the most courageous things you can do.

• • •

We hear it said so many times in so many different situations. In one way or another, the phrase "the game" is repeated to us through various channels. Be it book titles, catch phrases, or figures of speech, we routinely hear things like "winning the game," "beat the game," "game of thrones," and "hate the game, not the player." (By the way, there's literally a book titled *The Game of Life and How to Play It*. I haven't read it yet.) It's no surprise that many people feel as if they're fighting an uphill battle, one in which they may gain some ground but couldn't ever possibly win.

So, what is the point? Why even bother if there's no chance of "winning?" If you're following the societal rules and norms in order to be an upstanding citizen, does that make you a player? If, instead, you seek anarchy and chaos, does that mean you're individualistic and unique, or are you simply playing a different game?

If sports were your passion, your purpose, your calling, but a life in athletics is no longer in your future, how do you move on? Or should you move on? My transition was a choice, and for many, that's not the case. Injury, illness, personnel cuts, inability to reach the next level, and major life changes beyond our control are also endings to athletic careers. Shouldn't the privilege of being able to choose make it easier? In my case, not so much. And I'm willing to bet that there are many others that chose to quit but struggle to transition.

My hope is that regardless of your reason for transitioning from a life of athletics to the "real world," this book will help guide you to understanding more about yourself and find a life full of purpose. Even if you've never had suicidal thoughts or if your transition was relatively easy, if you've played a sport and sometimes catch yourself thinking "what if," I believe this book will be beneficial to you. But it won't be everyone's cup of tea.

The goal of this book is to help you:

1. Understand more about yourself.
2. Understand FEAR and how to overcome it.
3. Assess and improve your "coachability."
4. Understand the role of money and finances in your happiness.
5. Learn the freeing effect of self-denial.
6. Gain a new perspective of competition and comparisons.
7. Understand happiness and consider a different perspective.
8. Grow in your relationship with God.

CHAPTER 2

WHERE WE ARE

Sports and Western Culture

The youth sports industry has grown to an estimated $15 billion—yes, with a "B"—per year *business*. Parents buy the best gear, get their kids on the best team with the best coaches, and spare no expense to get them the training and opportunities to set themselves apart from the rest of the little Mike Trouts-in-training.

The Sports and Fitness Industry Association (SFIA) estimated that there were 21.47 million kids between ages six and seventeen actively participating in sports in 2011. But what's the likelihood that these millions of kids will make a career out of it? Or even make it to the next level? Here are the NCAA's estimates for a high school athlete making it to Divisions I, II, and III in their respective sport:

	Overall % HS to NCAA	% HS to Div. I	% HS to Div. II	% HS to Div. III
Men				
Baseball	**7.3%**	2.2%	2.2%	2.9%
Basketball	**3.4%**	1.0%	1.0%	2.9%
Football	**7.1%**	2.8%	1.8%	2.5%
Soccer	**5.5%**	1.3%	1.5%	2.7%
Women				
Softball	**5.5%**	1.7%	1.6%	2.2%
Basketball	**4.0%**	1.2%	1.2%	1.6%
Volleyball	**3.9%**	1.2%	1.1%	1.6%
Soccer	**7.1%**	2.4%	1.9%	2.8%

Don Sabo, a professor at D'Youville College in Buffalo, surveyed 2,185 students between grades 3 and 12 and found that 61% of male students and 34% of female students said sports are a big part of *who they are*. That means millions and millions of kids and young adults lose at least a portion of their identity when they have to give up competitive, organized sports.

This book won't offer the secret to developing kids into top 2-percenters. Instead, we'll dig into what happens after it's all over and what we can do to discover a new love, a new purpose, and a new identity. We'll look at the key components of a happy life and how we can maintain a state of happiness regardless of our station.

Conditioning

When kids show a particularly acute level of skill at an early age, they're often highly regarded and praised for their "talent." We tend to focus on their God-given abilities and tell them over and over again what a "natural" they are. But is that the message we should be sending them? Do we notice when a kid at the supermarket picks up an item on the floor and puts it back on the shelf? What about the teenager who chooses to stay away from drugs and alcohol even though most of her friends are using? Do we praise them the same way we would praise the kid who sunk a game winning 3-pointer or the one who drives in the go-ahead run? Do we tell them that we're proud of them in everyday situations like we would after they gave it their best in their uniform?

Think about when you felt most accomplished as a child. If you're reading this book, it probably has something to do with sports. But I guarantee there are other memories you can dig up that don't involve sports at all. Did you protect another person from a bully? Did you complete a difficult project on your own? Did you mow the grass just right and get a hearty handshake from your dad saying how great the yard looked? That's a big one.

I bring up the focus on athletic accomplishments in our youth for a reason: we need to recognize that if we don't praise our kids today for the things they do outside of sports, they can develop an unhealthy or misguided view of true success and accomplishment. However, I also want to point out how we as individuals may have filtered the praise and attention we received as youngsters. Although our parents, teachers, and coaches may have praised us for great things we did outside of sports, we may have processed it differently than the praise we received for the great things we did in sports. Why is that?

A simple explanation would be that people, inadvertently or not, praise with more passion for sports accomplishments. That passion is communicated more with body language and actions than with the words people use. It's obvious, even to young folks, how people really feel about the praise they're giving. After that walk-off home run, you can bet that coach is going to run up to Junior and give him a fire-eyed bear hug with a Ric Flair "Woooo!"

It's a little different when Junior brings home his report card and shows Mom his "A" in Math that he struggled to achieve. The "great job, buddy!" just doesn't quite hit the same.

We've been accidentally (for the most part) conditioned to believe sports accomplishments are most important because of the way those closest to us react to them.

So how do we transition from a life of sports to a life we love regardless of our occupation, income, lifestyle, marital status, and so on?

By refocusing on the *foundation*.

Building from the Ground Up

If we don't like something about ourselves or the current status of our lives, we need to improve the situation. We do that by taking an honest look at ourselves and assessing where we are. Next, we decide where we want to be. Then, we can begin to incrementally improve those aspects of our lives by taking decisive action. Be prepared for a marathon, not a sprint.

I used to spend too much time watching "influencers" on social media. To be fair, they're folks that I admired for their entrepreneurial and fitness achievements and, for the most part, offered solid advice on how to get where they are. For a long time, I thought if I could learn enough from them, I could be more like them. Maybe that's partially true, but the real reason I spent so much time watching their content is because they've achieved what I dream of achieving. I was living my dream through them, and that's not really living.

If I'm honest with myself, I was not working toward my goals by doing the things that needed to be done, and I was using the guise of "research" in the form of YouTube videos and Instagram posts. Don't get me wrong, you can find some great content on those platforms, but sooner or later, you have to take decisive action. The scary part is learning how to take that action because you will fail in one way or another, but the beauty is that the failures are our best teachers. Forget the negative voice in your head discouraging you from even trying. It's a scam. We've been conditioned to believe that one failure means we've lost, that we're a loser.

The people at the top have discovered the secret: winning is simply taking action. The players at the top know it. The speculative sideliners spinning their wheels know it too but are just too afraid of the *first* failure. Could it go really bad? Maybe. But could it also go really good? Absolutely. Most of the time, we let our imagination grossly overexaggerate how bad it could get. We focus too much on the bad and find it very, very easy to create excuses as to why we can't take the first step toward our dream.

But more on that in the "FEAR" chapter.

Once you've decided on the direction and action, be consistent. You've done the research, and you know what needs to be done. Now do it over and over and over again. Be *diligent*.

CHAPTER 3

CLARITY

One of the most powerful bits of wisdom my dad tried to impart on me was this simple statement: "It's all in your head." At the time, he was simply explaining to my seventeen-year-old self that swallowing a small pill is simple when you get over your own perceived limitations. (No, I couldn't swallow pills until I was a junior in high school. Don't laugh.) But there was something in the way he said those words that made it evident he wasn't just talking about being able to get over my fear of choking.

Many years later, those words have become a daily reminder. No matter your trials, no matter your circumstance, no matter your worries, fears, and doubts, your perception greatly affects the manner in which you approach each situation. Here's the thing about perception: you can *change* it. In his book *The Seven Habits of*

Highly Effective People, Steven Covey calls this change of perception a "paradigm shift."

When we stop to think about why we are where we are in life, we tend to think about what has happened *to* us instead of how we *see* life and the world around us. The truth is the world is different for everyone. We really do all "live in our own little world." Can you improve your life by shifting your paradigm? First, we have to understand what a paradigm is. It's not simply a perspective.

A paradigm is what we hold as an absolute truth within our mind.

> A paradigm is a mental program that has almost exclusive control over our habitual behavior, and almost all of our behavior is habitual. (Bob Proctor)

A paradigm controls:

1. Our perception
2. Our use of time
3. Our creativity
4. Our effectiveness
5. Our productivity
6. Our logic
7. Our ability to earn money

Priorities

Too many times when we want to see a change in ourselves, we want the light bulb to turn on. We want a permanent switch to flip. But we often don't realize that it takes small, incremental changes over a longer period of time to experience lasting change. We *want* a quick fix and instant gratification, but what we really *need* is to relax, take a deep breath, and prepare for a long, fruitful journey. Our growth is in the uncomfortable climb.

Priorities are where we begin our change journey. Think about the things you would like to change about yourself. A few things I'd like to change would be my physique, my organizational skills, and my committed time with family.

What priorities should I focus on with each of these desired changes? For physique, I should obviously prioritize exercise and healthy eating habits along with a consistent sleep schedule. Becoming more organized may be a little trickier. Since I'm not a naturally organized person, I have to spend more time in repetition of organizational habits. I should also pay very close attention to how organized people operate with certain tasks. Asking them questions and asking for help should also be priorities if I really want to improve.

What about family time? I think ground rules should be discussed and agreed upon with my wife before

Playing the Game

implementing big changes. However, smaller things like putting my phone on silent before I walk in the door, intentionally talking with each of my children about their day for at least ten minutes, letting them pick a game to play or a book to read, telling my wife something I admire or appreciate about her, and cuddling and showing affection are all things I can prioritize when I'm home to make sure my family knows I love them.

Visualization

Coaches often tell their players to visualize themselves making great things happen. For example, a basketball player sees herself sink the game winning shot, or a football player imagines himself making an unbelievable catch in the endzone.

Before every high school football game, our coaches sent us to a dark, quiet place for fifteen minutes. There was no talking, no horseplay, and no distractions allowed. We were to close our eyes and see ourselves getting the job done on the field. The offensive lineman would visualize burying the defender, receivers would visualize blowing past the opponent and making the catch, and linebackers would visualize reading the queues and making a huge hit. Regardless of the position, visualization was the most important part of pregame preparation.

Life is the same way. Before we attack a goal or go after a dream, we have to see ourselves achieving it. Some of us do this naturally, while others struggle a great deal. We all have an inner voice that influences us one way or another. It's called our subconscious. Although our subconscious thoughts aren't something we're acutely aware of, we receive clues about what we've been conditioned to believe by paying attention to our feelings, especially when standing at the bottom of the mountain looking up. If we feel a sense of confidence and excitement, our subconscious is telling us that we have what it takes to accomplish the goal. If we feel discouraged or anxious, our subconscious has been negatively conditioned. Here's the beautiful thing: you can influence and recondition your subconscious thoughts through visualization and filtering.

Filtering

We're a product of what we've allowed to permeate our minds. Think about what you watch on TV, what your group of friends talk about, what you read on Facebook, what advertisements tell you, and what you were told growing up about your talents, abilities, or intelligence. We choose what we allow into our minds. So, why are we leaving the door to our mind wide open for others to come in and dump their garbage? Filtering the massive amount of information that is presented to us on a daily basis might seem like a daunting task, but avoiding sources of negativity altogether alleviates much of the burden.

When I listen to political news for too long, I start to feel low, discouraged, and negative. I don't enjoy conflict, and it makes me squirm when people treat each other with that level of disrespect. The easy solution for me is to not turn on the TV in the first place! I would rather spend my free time reading a book or working on an outdoor project. Sometimes we're in a position where we can't control the information coming at us.

I was in a doctor's office one morning a few months ago, and there was a TV in the waiting room broadcasting a heated debate between two politicians I'd never heard of. I'm not even sure what they were arguing about because I tuned it out as soon as I walked in. Maybe it was something important, but, in that situation, I didn't need to get worked up about whatever it was they were so passionate about. I chose to tune out the garbage. If I had paid attention to the dispute, my feelings and emotions would have been altered and could have affected the conversation with my doctor and everyone else I was with that day. Everyone receives information in their own way, but you need to recognize the triggers that cause you to have negative feelings. When you can't avoid the situation, consciously choose to disregard the information as impertinent to your growth, and simply don't accept it as truth.

Clarity

Do you know someone who seems to have it all figured out? Do they exude confidence, a sense of purpose, focus, and success? I'm willing to bet that the same person seems to be unusually happy. Maybe they're not always chipper, but when you think about that person, you get a sense of warmth and inspiration. They are great conversationalists and seem to think through tough situations easily. How are they so clear on everyday decisions and just life in general?

Back in high school, I had two friends who were very clear on their career goals. One was an excellent cross-country runner, and the other wasn't all that interested in sports. They were both very intelligent individuals but not the valedictorian-type when it came to grades. The cross-country star decided he would be a fighter pilot, and the other decided he would be a storm chaser/meteorologist. They were always very clear on their goals and were happy to share information about their passions when asked. Throughout high school, they quietly worked toward their dreams and prepared for the next step.

Although one was an athlete and the other wasn't, they possessed uncannily similar personality traits in other regards. Both were generally happy people, both were very friendly and kind to everyone around them, both were well spoken and direct when carrying on a conversation, and neither one was afraid to stand their ground and defend their position in an argument but weren't too proud to concede when the evidence proved otherwise. But the most noticeable commonality between the two was the fire in their eyes. You know the look, the one that communicates hunger for life, a sense of purpose. They were very clear about who they were and the direction they were going.

Today, it's no surprise that Ashton is an accomplished fighter pilot in the United States Air Force and Colt is the reincarnation of Bill Paxton's character "Bill Harding" from the 1996 movie *Twister*. By the way, Colt is also an accomplished photographer and takes amazing weather photos. Check out his work at https://fineartamerica.com/profiles/1-colt-forney.

I have long been jealous of how seemingly effortless it was for Ashton and Colt to be so clear about what they would do when they grew up. And now they've actually done it! Like so many others, my vision was blurry. I couldn't see myself doing anything other than sports. Certain industries and trades seemed interesting, but isn't life really just about making a ton of money and becoming relatively well known? I mean, the most memorable people in history were rich and famous, right?

The pain from my lack of clarity was self-inflicted because I was focused on the wrong goal. There's nothing inherently wrong with building wealth and becoming famous, but that shouldn't be the focus. It could be a by-product of pursuing your passion.

You hear so many motivational speakers say, "Do what you're passionate about." Or "find your calling, your purpose, and do that!" Well, what if you don't have a clue about what you really want? How do you pursue a calling that hasn't called? What if you're interested in many things, and there's really no clear front-runner? I've been there. Those questions haunted me for half of my life. I thought God had designed a very clear purpose for me and it was my job to find out what that purpose was. So why couldn't I figure it out? Why was I so unhappy? Because God doesn't design most of us for one specific worldly purpose. He designed us for more than that.

I wasn't designed to be an athlete or a banker or an insurance agent or a father or [you fill in the blank]. God designed us to be curious and inquisitive, to try new things, to learn and grow, and to be beautifully unique. Much of our lack of clarity comes from accepting a clouded societal view of what we *should* do instead of what we *enjoy* doing. Please don't misinterpret what I mean here. I'm not saying we should sit on a beach drinking piña coladas 24/7. What I am saying is that when we are able to clarify what we're interested in, what we enjoy doing, and understand our own talents and gifts, we can begin to develop a sense of direction for our lives. I believe God wants us to be happy, but I also believe He wants us to be productive. When we can combine our passion with productivity, the possibilities are truly astounding.

So, what's the secret to clarity? It's the understanding that you don't have to find the one specific occupation, title, position, or craft that will give your life meaning. You are enough just by being yourself. The secret is learning about yourself and knowing who you are, not what you think other people want you to be. Sometimes that's not as easy as we'd like it to be.

Who am I? I'm a child of God, made in His image. There may be others like me, but none are exactly like me. I was fearfully and wonderfully made.

Ashton and Colt seemed to have it all figured out at an early age. Maybe they did, but if you asked them, I'm sure they would tell you sometimes they felt like imposters, like they didn't belong. Acquiring clarity doesn't mean you'll know what to do 100% of the time. Being clear is about how you process your thoughts.

My wife and I are similar in many ways, but she would agree with me that opposites certainly attract. She tends to be concise and to the point, while I tend to overanalyze the details. She would say I'm a good mediator, but I envy her ability to respond quickly to various circumstances. For me to develop clarity, I have to intentionally focus on my thoughts and organize them into actionable categories. If you're like me, your mind runs 1,000 miles per hour, and you have 13 different (and often unrelated) thoughts occurring at the same time. For me to develop clarity requires a lot of effort. I must mentally slow down and choose the thought that makes the most sense in the current situation. Then, I focus on that thought and develop it into a response that aligns with the goal at hand.

For example, writing this book has forced me to focus on one category at a time. When writing this chapter, I had thoughts about other chapters, work, religion, the current political climate, my wife and family, household chores, my health and fitness, my favorite football team, an upcoming trip I don't feel prepared for, and a million projects I have yet to complete. And if I didn't take those thoughts captive and refocus on the goal at hand, I would have let my mind wander and my mission would have been delayed, if not derailed. Clarity, for me, is setting a goal, understanding what's required to achieve that goal, and *acting* on those requirements.

One. Step. At a time.

CHAPTER 4

FEAR

The legendary motivational speaker Zig Ziglar stated that fear is an acronym that stands for *false evidence appearing real*. When we stop and think about *why* we are fearful of something, we often discover the truth in Zig's statement. Most of the time, our fear is expressed in the form of anxiety and stress. Whether it's stressing about how someone will react to a decision we've made or worrying about how we're going to complete a long list of tasks before a deadline, we've all felt the sting of fear.

The thing about fear is that whatever we're fearful of hasn't actually happened yet. We play out terrible scenarios in our mind because we're focused on the negative possibilities.

• • •

Finding Truth

> To the Jews who had believed him, Jesus said, "If you hold to my teaching, you are really my disciples. Then you will know the truth, and the truth will set you free." (John 8:31-32)

We've all heard the last line of this scripture many times, but what was Jesus really saying when He says the truth will set us free? Free from what? And is it as simple as adhering to the teachings of Jesus, being a disciple, and living by His word?

Let's take a look at the opposite of freedom for a moment: slavery. The definition of slavery is "submission to a dominating influence." Here in the United States, we are all free to live how we choose, that is, where we live, what we eat, where/if we attend church, how we earn a living, what we wear, what we say, and so on. So how does slavery, or "submission to a dominating influence," apply to us? Jesus wasn't talking about our physical freedom. He was talking about the mental and spiritual oppression we inflict upon ourselves. Maybe you already knew that, but let's dig a little deeper.

What does self-inflicted mental and spiritual oppression look like? You're probably a mile ahead of me. Yes, it's FEAR. But what are we afraid of? Philosophers, neurologists, scientists, and others have their own ideas about fear. Some believe there are as many as fifty types of fear, but for the sake of simplicity, let's consolidate them into four primary fears:

1. Fear of failure
2. Fear of insignificance
3. Fear of guilt
4. Fear of success

Fear of Failure

We're all very familiar with the fear of failing. Whenever there's risk involved, no matter how small, we hear that little voice cautioning us to stay away from the thing that could cause us to stumble. We begin to feel uncomfortable and think of all the reasons why we won't be successful. We think about the ridicule we'll receive from our peers, bosses, or family as a result of the failure. We think about the time that will have been wasted and the "loser" label on our forehead.

The fear of failure can cause us to chronically procrastinate. Fear causes us to question whether the outcome is worth the action.

> "What if I screw up this project and the company loses a fortune?"

"What if all the prospects I call today say 'no' like they all did yesterday?"

"What if I decide to serve my spouse by giving them 100% of myself and it's not reciprocated?"

Whether we realize it or not, fear causes us to slip into a state of comfort or complacency. We find a safe zone and settle in. We think, *Hey, this isn't so bad. I think I'll stay right here. I mean, after all, if I put myself out there and try for something better, I could mess up and end up worse off than I am now.*

I like what former Navy SEAL, now ultra-marathon runner, David Goggins has to say about comfort: "Our whole life is set up in the path of least resistance. We don't want to suffer. We don't want to feel discomfort. So the whole time, we're living our lives in a very comfortable area. There's no growth in that."

Discomfort is scary. It's unfamiliar territory that we're unsure how to navigate. Our centuries-old survival instincts cause us to subconsciously choose the least risky option. Discomfort is our mind's way of telling us that the current path could lead to our demise.

David Goggins is a "paragon of grit," a phrase coined by author Angela Duckworth in her groundbreaking book *Grit: The Power of Passion and Perseverance* which we'll discuss later. Goggins epitomizes passion and perseverance. If you haven't heard his story, you should google him. Fair warning: he's not shy about speaking his mind, and his dialogue isn't appropriate for younger audiences. However, his message, story, and drive to continuously grow and live with the purpose of pushing himself mentally, physically, and emotionally far beyond the perceived limitations of human capability are awe inspiring, to say the least.

David Goggins is not afraid to fail.

Fear of failure causes self-doubt. Self-doubt can be one of the biggest hindrances to personal growth and success. So how do you beat it? By developing the clarity to tune into your inner wisdom. I used to think clarity was something that I would get someday when life wasn't so hectic. When things calmed down and I could catch my breath, maybe I would meditate and it would just happen. Now I know clarity is a skill that can be learned and developed. Think about this for a second: when you consider how productive you are throughout a typical day, what score would you give yourself on a scale of 1–10? Honestly.

We know what needs to be done we just tend to avoid doing it. How do we overcome this procrastination and lack of productivity? Develop confidence. And no, confidence is not a personality trait. It's a skill that can be learned. So how do we develop confidence?

1. Learn how to say "no" (boundaries).
2. Align your actions with your values and goals.
3. Be a fearless negotiator.
4. Learn self-control. (This ties into the chapter on "Self-Denial.")

Self-control could possibly be the no. 1 skill in today's world. Think about our entitled society. We've become obsessed with convenience, immediate gratification, never being told "no," and spewing garbage throughout social media. Being a person with dignified self-control is becoming a rarity in our culture.

Confidence is more than just positive thinking. While positive thinking is necessary for building confidence, it only takes you part of the way. You must *take action* and try the thing despite your fear.

> If you have a problem that can be solved with action, you don't have a problem. (Mel Robbins)

Mel Robbins' take on competency and fear of failure:

Confidence Competency Loop
    Try something.
    Either succeed or survive.
    Learn something.
    Build skills.

Develop competency.
Develop confidence.
Repeat.

Fear of Failure Loop (unsure, nervous, rejection, overwhelmed)
Overthink.
Doubt yourself.
Repeat.

* In order to end the fear of failure loop, you must insert a good habit loop, that is, *take action!*

What is confidence? The *decision* to try.
What is self-doubt? The *decision* not to.

The four traps of self-doubt are as follows:

1. Hesitating
    - Triggered by uncertainty.
    - Waiting.
    - Overthinking.
    - Wanting your work to be "perfect."
2. Hiding
    - Triggered by fear (avoid people, tasks).

3. Hypercritical
   - Triggered from past failures.
   - Argue against yourself.
   - You focus on the reasons why you can't.
   - You fixate on what could go wrong.
   - Your stress has an edge.
4. Helplessness
   - Triggered by insecurity.
   - Actively play the victim.
   - You have all the excuses in the book.

When to Change

In any area of your life you want to change, there is one fact that remains constant: you're never going to feel like it. We keep waiting to do something until we feel like it, but the wait will never end. We may have moments of motivation, but the "right" moment is now.

Scientists define "activation energy" as the force required to get you to change what you're doing on auto-pilot to doing something new. Your parents made you do the things you didn't feel like doing when you were a kid. But when you become an adult and are supposed to be self-sufficient, it's difficult to accept the self-discipline necessary to become what you want to be.

It's simple but not easy. You must force yourself to do the things that need to be done. Anything that's a break from your routine will require force. The routine is killing you. Dissatisfaction is a signal that your most basic needs are not being met, that is, the need for exploration and growth. The only way to get it is by forcing yourself to be uncomfortable. Get out of your head, get past your feelings, and get outside your comfort zone.

Fear of Insignificance

Sigmund Freud believed that *everything* we do springs from two motives:

1. The sex urge
2. A desire to be great

Another renowned psychologist, Dr. John Dewey, believed that "the deepest urge in human nature is the desire to be important." We have an ingrained longing to achieve great things, to be remembered, and to make a lasting impact. When we see ourselves in a negative light, without the hope of achieving anything of significance, we can become entrenched in the fear of insignificance. Think about the biggest questions we ask ourselves: *What is my purpose? Who am I meant to be?*

We all feel like we're meant to be something special. The word "special" indicates exclusivity — uniqueness; meaning, very few are awarded the term.

The desire of significance, or to be someone of importance, can cause us more harm than good if not controlled. If we do not organize our thoughts and set firm goals, our desires can lead us down dead-end road after dead-end road. Think of the goals you'd like to achieve. What have you started in the past but never finished? Do you, like me, tend to get a noble idea of something you'd like to accomplish only to toss it aside after a couple weeks? This is our inherent longing to do something of significance, but we become distracted too easily.

I "decided" in the past that I was going to learn guitar, piano, sign language, and Spanish. I've become proficient in none of them. Why? Because as soon as I started, I became distracted by less important things that required less effort.

When we feel the sting of rejection, our fear of insignificance can surge back into our thoughts. We all feel rejected at times. But think about what rejection means: someone doesn't feel that your idea, need, effort, skill set, and so on are worth their time and attention. Sounds harsh, but it's *not you* they're rejecting. Now, I know that we can be rejected entirely. Sometimes people just flat don't like us, and they choose to dismiss us altogether. Sometimes we don't quite fit in, and the rejection is an unspoken understanding among our classmates, coworkers, peers, or even our family. I'm naturally a people pleaser, so rejection is extremely hard for me to handle sometimes.

How does rejection affect us, and how do we overcome it? First, we must understand what rejection does to us mentally. When you're rejected, it attacks your core. You feel an assault on your identity, so you rush to shore up what you feel defines you. This could be your material possessions, your career, your title, your reputation, your athletic accomplishments, or your perceived image of yourself. Insecurity causes you to believe that your identity comes from these outside things instead of what's already inside you. By believing your identity is derived from these outside things, you leave yourself vulnerable to manipulation. God wants your identity to be established on your relationship with Him. With that kind of foundation, how could we falter?

When I was working in insurance, I had a client tell me they were closing their accounts and switching to another agency. I'm a competitive person, so for me, losing an account to a competitor is hard to swallow, regardless of the reason. But after a little digging, I discovered the reason they were switching was because they didn't feel like they were receiving the level of service they deserved from me. That one cut me deep. I pride myself on the level of service I provide all my clients, and to be rejected by

Playing the Game

one of them was a total gut punch. My first instinct was to tell them off.

I gave myself a moment to think about how I wanted to respond. If I was being honest with the client and myself, he was right. I could have done more to make him feel like a valued client. Instead, he felt like a second-rate customer. I took his rejection personally, but it wasn't *me* he was rejecting. It was the service I provided or lack thereof. Still, my initial reaction was to find validation from others of the quality of my service. I needed to feel like the client was wrong about me. My reputation had taken a beating, and I needed it to be mended. My first action was to complain to my coworker about how unbelievable this client was being. I mean, who would think that I'm not doing my best? Or worse, what if he thinks I'm doing my best, but it's not good enough? I made a strong case and sold my side hard.

However, after my short-lived pity party, I took an honest look at my recent history of account servicing. Could I honestly tell myself I had done the best job I could for all my customers? Was the overall workload and craziness of ever-increasing new business prospects a valid excuse for neglecting to cultivate valued customer relationships?

No and no.

When thinking about that client now and the fact that he was brutally honest with me, I'm thankful for the learning experience it provided. Rejection is never easy, but when we look at it through new lenses, it can provide powerful lessons and insights about ourselves.

Rejection distorts our way of looking at others and life in general. We can reason and develop intellectual thoughts with our brain, but we interpret life through our feelings or "heart." When you're wounded, you'll question what people mean when they make certain comments, whether it's a comment of correction or simple misinterpretation of a simple statement. That questioning will result in the inevitable answer of "they don't like me."

This distorted view will cause us to ask why we aren't receiving the same blessings or praise that other people seem to receive. We ask, "Why don't I have that? That should be happening to me." And our depression will cause us to not rejoice in others' triumphs and successes.

Rejection can hinder your ability to receive from God. Everything we receive from God comes by faith, and when faith is in your heart, you believe you will receive His blessings. Rejection makes you think God will do it for other people but not you. You believe that you are the exception to the rule. Rejection has stolen your belief that you should receive good things in your life.

With rejection comes unbelief. The spirit of rejection can cause us to condition ourselves subconsciously to believe we're not worthy. So then, how do we overcome the spirit of rejection? Change your mind about abandonment and rejection to understand that God's spirit is within us and we are beloved children of God. We think "God is up there" when, in reality, His spirit is within us always. We are carriers of the presence of God. How can we be rejected when God is always with us?

To be a healthy, happy person, we have to set boundaries with those around us, and we need to respect the boundaries of others as well. Sometimes what we interpret as rejection is actually just a boundary that someone is unwilling to forfeit. Maybe their communication of that boundary could have been delivered in a better way, but understand that we often feel rejected unnecessarily.

Fear of Guilt

It's funny how the twinge of guilt can quickly trigger a defensive response within us that excuses the act. We have an intense urge to explain our way out of the mess we put ourselves in. Think about the *very first* example of guilt in the Bible. Even though Eve handed him the forbidden fruit, Adam knew what it was. And when God asked him what he had done, he tried to pass the blame to Eve! Sometimes, we're even tempted to lie, to others and ourselves, in order to avoid the awful, gut-wrenching feeling of guilt. Why do we struggle so much with guilt?

Guilt is a natural response to the realization that we've done, or are about to do, something wrong. When God designed us in His infinite wisdom, He gifted us with guilt so we could recognize our wrong, learn from it, and avoid doing it again in the future. Guilt is a terrible feeling, but God designed it that way on purpose. We don't like bad feelings, and we try to only do things that give us good feelings.

Guilt brings shame. Without repenting, we can live in the fog of shame much longer than we need to. In Psalm 25, David prays for deliverance from shame and forgiveness of the sins of his youth. What is the solution to overcoming guilt and shame?

> He guides the **humble** in what is right and teaches them his way. All the ways of the LORD are loving and faithful toward those who **keep the demands of his covenant**. (Psalm 25:9–10, bold added for emphasis)

If we humble ourselves before the Lord and follow His commandments, He will lead us past our guilt, and we will avoid future situations that cause us to feel guilty.

Living in our guilt causes us to think about ourselves too much. We focus on our mistakes rather than our victories. Self-focus is fertilizer on fear, like gas on a fire. Shift your focus to others and how you can help them, and your fear of guilt starts to vanish.

Fear of Success

What's the hardest part of pursuing a worthwhile project, goal, or dream? It's not the actual "doing" of the thing; it's taking the first step. Why is that? When we visualize taking a step, it seems like something so incredibly simple it's hard to understand how one *couldn't* do it. But the buildup to the actual act of taking the step involves your psyche. We stop ourselves before we even start. It's not that we don't think we can take the first step, then the next and so on; it's that we're afraid we'll actually succeed at accomplishing the mission.

The fear of success is actually stronger than the fear of failure.

Let me explain.

We tend to think of success as the acquisition of more money, more recognition, more respect, and maybe an "easier" life. The truth is success comes at a price, and we are fearful of whether it's a price we want to pay. With exercise and diet, for example, we fantasize about having six-pack abs and shredded arms, but is it really the time commitment and nutritional discipline we're afraid of? Could it possibly be that we're afraid of developing a strict regimen because it may prevent us from spending as much time with our friends or having to decline the cake and ice cream at birthday parties, or it may cause us to miss out on beers after work with the guys?

What if you exercised regularly and maintained excellent physical shape? Could it be that we're afraid some of our friends won't like the new, transformed person we've become? Think about how you feel when people you know improve themselves in some way. Outwardly, we're supportive and encouraging, but how do you really feel about their transformation? Does it remind you of your own lack of success? Does it cause feelings of disappointment? Do you want to avoid that person because of those feelings?

We fear success because it ostracizes us from others that don't want to change. Our fear of success in fitness endeavors isn't because of the time commitment or physical pain we'll experience; it's that our success will lead to new opportunities, and we're unsure about changing our lives because we've grown accustomed and *comfortable*. The same is true in our spiritual, financial, emotional, intellectual, social, and occupational journeys.

We need to be challenged to improve. Growing is uncomfortable, but that short-term pain or unpleasantness will lead to riches in each position of life. (Be careful not to think of riches meaning only money here.)

My favorite definition of success is the following:

> Success is the progressive realization of a worthy ideal. (Earl Nightingale)

Earl Nightingale was a radio speaker who produced radio shows for over three decades. The previous quote was taken from one of his most famous recordings called *The Strangest Secret*. Go to YouTube, and search for it now. Listen to it in its entirety. This recording was originally produced in 1956. It is considered one of the pioneering events for motivational speaking and personal development.

Success isn't a destination; it's the journey, the process of taking the next step forward on the path to reaching your goal. The journey isn't always easy, and it isn't always pleasant. But success is moving forward despite the setbacks, despite the frustrations, despite the disappointments.

We fear success because of the unknown. We fear success because of the sacrifices that we will inevitably be faced with. The secret is that they seem so insignificant when we look back from the other side.

CHAPTER 5

Coachability

Kole was the classic coaches' dream in every sport. When the coach spoke, his eyes were fixed on theirs, and he nodded his head along with the points of the speech. He didn't just listen, he absorbed everything they said. As a grade schooler, he wasn't the biggest, the fastest, the strongest, or the most talented, but his hustle was second to none. He gave every ounce possible to get the job done.

In junior high and early high school, Kole was assigned to the grunt work: battling it out in the trenches on the gridiron and was used for his defensive tenacity on the basketball court. But each year, and each summer in-between, he kept absorbing instruction and kept working harder than anyone to hone his knowledge and skill, as well as build his body, to perform at the highest level possible.

Our senior year, at 5'8" and 170 pounds, Kole was the starting middle linebacker and captain of the defense as well as the starting left guard on the offensive line. He was the most technically sound member of the team and knew each players' role for every play. He was a pulling guard, so he often led me through the hole and blasted the nearest defender, making my job as a running back much easier.

What was most impressive about Kole's senior campaign was the number of tackles he tallied. Kole had a nose for the ball, and it felt like he was a part of every tackle on defense. Looking at the stats, I'd say that's not far off. He finished the year with 176 total tackles in our 11-game campaign. Oh, and by the way, he missed a game for concussion protocol. We went 8-3 that year, so out of the 10 games he played, he averaged 17.6 tackles per game. The NFL record for most tackles per game in a season belongs to Ray Lewis. He averaged 8.6 in 2002 (https://www.statmuse.com. Accessed April 19, 2023). I know 2A Kansas football and the NFL are very different, but that's impressive nonetheless.

The point of this story is that being coachable prepares us for the long haul. Being coachable doesn't remove all the obstacles, but it does teach us humility and patience—two virtues paramount to long-term success.

Are You Coachable?

We often hear about an athlete's level of talent in a particular sport and hear predictions of what their future holds. We see highlights and stats of the best athletes over and over again until they are committed to memory. Occasionally, we'll hear about their "coachability." Whether or not an athlete is coachable is essential to their long-term success, but it's even more important in the real world.

When your boss tells you that you need improvement in a specific area of your job, what's your first reaction? Do you dispute their points and argue against them? Maybe you nod in agreement, but inside you're thinking, *This guy has no idea what he's talking about!* Do you notice similarities in how you handled criticisms from coaches and how you now handle them from your leaders?

Great coaches made it easy to take instruction. They seemed to have that suave way of communicating that made you want to run through a brick wall for them. I'll admit that, for the most part, I've been extremely lucky with the coaches and supervisors I've had throughout my life. But the reality is that we don't get along with everyone. Sometimes, the person we directly report to is an impossible human being. Everything that spills out of their mouth is garbage, and we can hardly tolerate their presence, let alone accept corrective criticism from them.

But what's the solution? How do we improve our circumstances when it seems like we're playing a game with no chance of winning?

Start digging for gold.

Andrew Carnegie, the famous multimillionaire industrialist, at one time had 43 millionaires working for him. In the late 1800s, millionaires were very rare, so a reporter interviewed Mr. Carnegie to determine how he could have so many millionaires working for him. After telling the reporter that the men were not millionaires when they started working for him, Mr. Carnegie was asked how he could pay these men so much money for their services that they had become millionaires. He explained it beautifully in the following quote:

> Men are developed the same way gold is mined. When gold is mined, several tons of dirt must be moved to get an ounce of gold; but one doesn't go into the mine looking for dirt—one goes in looking for the gold.

I love that analogy. In this example, Carnegie is talking about developing employees, but "mining for gold" can be used in a multitude of other circumstances. Let's assume that your boss has given you constructive criticism. If you're like me, the fact that someone wants to correct you can be a hard pill to swallow. You might think that she's just picking on you or maybe that her criticism is totally unfounded. But take a deep breath, and take an honest look at what she said. Don't focus on her tone or strong words or her use of cliché terms like "constructive criticism." Instead, dig through all the dirt, and find the gold buried within. Try to put yourself in her position for a second.

I'll be honest. I struggle with coachability. Maybe it's my personality. Maybe I'm a thickheaded person with a strong will. Maybe I'm arrogant. Or maybe it's all in my head, and I just choose to be that way. Whatever the reason, this is an area I really have to work at improving. But I also believe that *knowing this about myself* makes it easier for me to humble myself and accept the guidance of others. We often confuse humility with submissiveness. In a way, we *are* submitting. We're submitting to the fact that we're not perfect and that we need instruction to develop our abilities. Too often, we're concerned with not having all the answers because we think our personal stock will decline or we'll have to acknowledge that we still have work to do. Maybe you had a coach, like I did, that repeated this line: "The work is never done." We will never reach the peak. That last bit might sound depressing, but it's really relieving. When we tie ourselves up in the perfectionist mindset, we set ourselves up for certain failure. But when we realize that even at our best we will never be perfect, we're able to focus on the true meaning of success. In Earl Nightingale's words, success is "the progressive realization of a worthy ideal." So, as long as we're working toward improving, even fractionally, we're successful. But we often take the failures and setbacks way too hard. Zig Ziglar said it best: "Failure is an event, not a person." Failure is the stepping stone to success.

Coachability, then, is simply your ability to accept advice that guides you to mitigate the mistakes and failures along the way. The people who coach you have often gone through very similar, if not the exact same, circumstances in the past and can help you avoid the mistakes they made. This could expedite your ascension to the level of accomplishment at which you're aiming and make the process much more enjoyable. However, having a great coach doesn't mean you won't mess up. It doesn't mean you won't struggle. It doesn't mean you get to skip the hard parts. Having a great coach (or coach*es*) simply means you have an incredible advantage in overcoming the difficulties when you face them.

In the real world, we sometimes refer to coaches as "mentors." These people are folks that we look up to, respect, or admire. They've accomplished the things we want to accomplish. They are the type of person we strive to be. They attract people, money, and positivity, among other things. They don't have to be everything we want to be, but they do have to be someone that possesses similar values and a moral compass. We don't always choose our coaches, but we do *always* choose our mentors. Sometimes, they become mentors before we realize they are, but solemn respect for a particular leader is usually a key indicator of a likely mentor.

Some of our mentors will be accessible through natural channels like church, civil service groups, or work. Occasionally, we are lucky enough to have unrestricted access to our mentors. More often, though, we have to ask someone we admire to agree to be our mentor. When this is the case, it's important to understand that the person has a life beyond their relationship with you. The amount of time they can give you may be very restricted, if they give any at all. Don't be discouraged if your number one choice for mentorship turns you down. If they're a quality choice, I guarantee you're not the only one asking for some of their time.

A counselor is very similar to a mentor. A counselor is anyone who can provide advice, wisdom, or any practical help for the effective achievement of a specific project, goal, or dream.[1] A relationship with a counselor is usually more formal and in a professional setting. They may require payment, or it may be worth offering to pay them

---

[1] *The Richest Man Who Ever Lived*, Steve K. Scott

for their time. Usually, folks that we'd like to have as counselors aren't associated with any part of our regular lives. If you believe a particular person would be very valuable to have in your corner, you may need to be assertive and willing to incentivize them to help you somehow. That's where counselors come in.

People that fit this description could be a psychologist or psychiatrist, a personal fitness trainer, a small business owner, a master tradesman, a financial advisor, an attorney, a pastor, a niche consultant, and many other professions.

CHAPTER 6

Financial Freedom

Highland, Kansas, is home to a unique community college experience. Highland Community College is the oldest college in Kansas and welcomes a few hundred new college students each fall. Many of the students experience a bit of culture shock when they come from cities like Houston, Atlanta, Miami, and Chicago and move to a town of 1,000 people, 25 miles from a "city" of roughly 75,000. In my mid-20s, I was employed at the local bank, and several HCC students would come in to set up checking accounts around the start of each semester.

One fall, a young woman came in and opened a new account. She was very personable and respectful. We set her up with checks and a checkbook ledger for tracking her expenses and deposits.

About two weeks after opening the account, she overdrew the account. By the time we were finally able to talk with her, she had written five "hot" checks. When we told her there weren't sufficient funds in her account to cover those checks, she responded with, "What do you mean!? I still have checks in my checkbook!"

The poor girl had never been taught how a checking account worked and genuinely believed that having a check meant she had purchasing power.

• • •

Money is a tool.

We tend to think that the game is to have the most, to get more of it than our peers (whom we view as competition). It's not really our fault; almost every message of success we hear from the materialistic world says more is better. When we focus on the money itself and not the purpose for which we need it, we will never have enough. Instead, see money for what it is: a tool that builds, fixes, and enables you to create.

Instead of thinking about a sum of money, think about the lifestyle you want. Try to set aside the materialism for a moment. Most people don't actually want the fancy stuff. They just want to be financially independent. What they want is *freedom*. Without understanding how money works and how to properly use it, you will never have true financial freedom.

Whether we like to admit it or not, money plays a major role in our daily lives and contributes directly to our happiness or lack thereof. Am I saying we need stockpiles of cash to be happy? No, but consider this:

John is forty years old. John makes $75,000 a year. He has no debt including a paid for home, six months' worth of expenses in a savings account and has $1.1 million in retirement accounts.

Larry is also forty years old. Larry also makes $75,000 a year. He has a $2,000 monthly mortgage payment that's three years into a thirty-year mortgage, $150 in his savings account, and $40,000 in credit card debt but does not have a retirement account because "you only live once and you might as well spend it while you're young."

Who do you think has less stress? (Let's assume neither is ignorant of the importance of financial independence.) Who has a firm grip on the steering wheel of financial freedom? What if they both lost their jobs? Which one is more equipped to ride out the storm?

The problem with this picture is that it only looks at the numbers on the surface. It doesn't show the hard work, sacrifice, diligence, and discipline required of John to get where he is financially. It doesn't show you their lifestyles,

Playing the Game

what they wear, what they drive, or what kind of house they live in.

Opportunity Cost

An often-overlooked aspect of financial literacy and financial freedom is knowing your opportunity costs. It's understanding what you are willing to forego to acquire the object you desire. Warren Buffett explains it by using a haircut analogy. Buffett has been going to the same barber nearly all his life and pays $18. As one of the wealthiest people in the world, he could obviously afford to pay much more for something "professional," but his perspective is much different than most. He says instead of spending $100 or more on a haircut, he would rather invest the difference. His opportunity cost could be that he may not have the nicest hair in a group of his peers. But he understands that his opportunity cost by getting a $100 haircut would be much more painful. Let's run the numbers:

- He would be spending an extra $82/month that he could be investing.
- For simplicity purposes, let's say he earns a 10% annual return, and let's not adjust for inflation.

- Mr. Buffett has been patronizing the same barber for a very long time, so let's look at a very long-term investment: sixty years.

How much money do you think Mr. Buffett would forego for the "better" haircut in this scenario? Remember $82/month, 10% return, 60 years.

$3,862,412!
For a stinking haircut!

That is opportunity cost.

Truly understanding your opportunity cost when making purchases can significantly improve the way you view needs vs. wants. Many things we blow our money on are unnecessary and take away from our greater goals. Think about the overpriced coffee you buy every morning or the daily lunch outings. Let's look at those numbers, shall we?

- $3 coffee + $12 lunch = $15/day
- $15 x 5 days/week = $75/week
- $75/week x 52 weeks/year - $3,900/year

Now, instead of the coffee and lunch, let's say we invest the $3,900.

- $3,900 @ 10% annual return for 30 years = $734,658
- $3,900 @ 10% annual return for 40 years = $2,055,325
- $3,900 @ 10% annual return for 50 years = $5,630,425
- $3,900 @ 10% annual return for 60 years = $15,308,370!

By the way, Albert Einstein called compounding interest the eighth wonder of the world. Time and consistency are your friends when it comes to saving and investing.

Opportunity cost works both ways. Sometimes, we have to consider our time and physical, emotional, and spiritual needs. My wife, Brittani, and I have three beautiful daughters, and we sacrifice a considerable amount of personal wants to make sure their needs are met. After our first was born, we worked hard to save and spent much more time at home just being a family. Apart from the occasional date night, we had not been away from our children for more than three nights.

I'm not a huge fan of travel, but Brittani loves to explore new places and has wanted to tour the southern plantations and east coast for a long time. When her 30th birthday was approaching, I knew I had a great opportunity to show her some love. Since it was her birthday and we hadn't been on a vacation with just each other in more than five years, I wanted it to be extra special. I researched bed and breakfasts, restaurants, tours, and shops to make it a trip to remember. Consequently, we also had a few projects for our home we were considering, namely, a new patio. When I totaled up the entire cost of the trip, I couldn't believe how much it was actually going to cost. So much for the patio!

But then I started to think about the opportunity cost. My wife and I have a great marriage. We have our trials like anyone else, but we genuinely love each other, and we truly, deeply trust one another. Even so, it was difficult not to feel distant without much one-on-one time. The patio would be a great addition to our home, but in my mind, the quality of our relationship is infinitely more important.

We spent a few days at a small B&B in Charleston, South Carolina, and had the best time together since our honeymoon. We talk about that trip often and agree that we'll go back someday. If we would have chosen the patio instead of the trip to Charleston, we would have had a nice addition to the house, but we would have missed the opportunity to connect and strengthen our relationship by focusing solely on one another and not the daily responsibilities that come with parenting.

Sidenote: Please don't assume spending lots of money equals a quality relationship. This trip was about connecting as husband and wife, and we could have done something less expensive to accomplish that, but we had the funds to take the trip, and both agreed it was a good idea. We are also very fortunate to have parents that were willing to watch the kids for several days.

Behavior vs. Knowledge

Much like diet and exercise, financial aptitude is much more about behavior than about knowledge. I subscribe to the 80/20 rule of finance, which is derived from the Pareto principle. The 80/20 rule assumes that 80% of financial success is based on our behaviors and 20% is based on knowledge.

Think about it: you know you should save a portion of every paycheck, and spending $8 on a cup of coffee is a little ridiculous. But if we've had a rough day, week, or month, we can easily ignore our knowledge and justify compromising our goals for immediate gratification. Our *behavior* can cause us to make poor decisions, depending on our *feelings*. For the most part, we know what we need to do, and how to behave, in order to have long-term financial success. Actually implementing those behaviors, on the other hand, is an entirely different challenge.

Sometimes, it's difficult to tell if we're doing what is prudent or if we're just following the crowd. Many times, the crowd is headed toward a cliff, but we feel safe because "everyone else is doing it." It's a false sense of security.

Think of the housing market crash of 2008. The crash of 2008 happened because people were buying more house than they could afford using subprime mortgages to finance them.

> A subprime mortgage is a home loan with a rate above prime, usually with an adjustable-rate provision, so when interest rates rise, individual mortgage payments increase. Some of these lending practices were predatory and resulted in tightened regulation in the mortgage lending industry.

People buying houses above their affordability limit justified the suspect behavior in many different ways:

"The housing market is the strongest it's ever been!"

"It doesn't matter what we pay for it, because it will just continue to appreciate!"

"The Joneses just bought a house for $500,000, and I know they make less than we do!"

"Our lender said we only qualify for the subprime adjustable-rate mortgage, but he said the economy is strong and it's unlikely that rates will increase too much."

Whenever we're about to do something financially foolish, we feel that twinge of apprehension. We hear that still small voice saying, "Pump the breaks, Junior. This may not be the right decision." Whether we decide to heed its warning is a question of our behavioral fortitude.

Developing the proper behaviors around finance doesn't take much understanding; it just requires diligence. King Solomon, considered by many to be the wisest and wealthiest man to ever live, wrote the Book of Proverbs in the Bible. He says the primary key to wealth and "riches" is diligence. If you haven't read Proverbs, I highly recommend it (and the rest of the Bible, for that matter). Also, Stephen Scott wrote a book on the wisdom of King Solomon and the lessons we can learn from his life. The book is titled *The Richest Man Who Ever Lived*, and it helps the reader answer the question, "How can I get rich?" Spoiler alert: it's almost entirely about behavior, and by the end of the book, you'll reframe the core question.

Financial freedom isn't about having more money. It's about developing habits that allow you to spend your time doing the things you're passionate about. If you haven't discovered your passions yet, keep searching. In the meantime, *behave* in a way that prepares you to seize the opportunity to pursue what drives you. Try new things, learn new skills, be a student of life, and soak up the experience. Money may come and go, but if you truly trust in God's provision and diligently pursue your goals, the things that truly matter will fall into place.

Remember, money is a tool, not the goal itself. Set real, tangible goals, and develop a clear plan on how to reach them. Learn how to use money, but more importantly, learn how to *behave* with money. Don't be afraid to ask for help.

> Plans fail for lack of counsel, but with many advisers they succeed. (Proverbs 15:22 NIV)

My caveat to this scripture is the source of counsel: be very careful taking advice from social media platforms such as YouTube, TikTok, and Facebook. Many "influencers" have great content, but many also create sensational material for likes and views. They can be charismatic and confident in their "advice," but if their information raises red flags, ask a lot of questions. My advice: talk to a real person, or several people, that has extensive experience in financial endeavors or business pursuits. Learn as much as possible from them.

CHAPTER 7

Self-Denial

> Then he said to them all: Whoever wants to be my disciple must deny themselves and take up their cross daily and follow me. For whoever wants to save their life will lose it, but whoever loses their life for me will save it. (Luke 9:23–24 NIV)

We don't like to think about denying ourselves of anything, especially when someone else suggests the notion. Sure, we've said no to soda and sweets during training, and even those of us who aren't Catholic are occasionally inspired to give up something we really enjoy for forty days during Lent. But the kind of self-denial I'm talking about goes much deeper.

It's a paradigm shift.

It's extremely difficult.

It's life-changing.

"Self-Denial" is the toughest part of the book for me to write, not in the sense of finding material and content, but in the sense of admitting mistakes and hard lessons. I've put a high price tag on image and reputation and have worked to make them as impeccable as possible. I'm not perfect, but isn't it ironic how we still strive for perfection and find it so difficult to admit our mistakes? We don't want others to think less of us. We don't want to lose our perceived "social status." We don't want to be outcast and downtrodden or "weird." So we cling to the false sense of security in the superficial image we broadcast to others.

Before getting into the weeds, it's important to point out something interesting about vices: We tend to think vices grip us so tightly that we can't move, that we're trapped. The reality is that *we* are gripping *them* so tightly and don't realize we can choose to let go. It reminds me of how African bushmen trap baboons to find water. The bushman will dig a hole in a tree or anthill big enough for the baboon to squeeze its arm through and drop melon seeds in the hole. The baboon, being an incurably curious creature, will reach in the hole and grab the seeds. His closed fist won't allow him to pull is arm out of the hole and the bushman will trap the baboon and feed it salt clumps to make it thirsty. Then the bushman will release the baboon and follow it to his water source.

Here's the key: if the baboon would just *let go of the melon seeds*, his arm would easily slide out of the hole, and he would escape before his captor could seize him.

The three important areas of self-denial in today's world are as follows:

1. Sexual impurity
2. Drugs and alcohol
3. Phone usage

Sexual Impurity

Like the majority of the men in our society (including Christians), I struggled with a pornography addiction until age twenty-four.

I was introduced to porn for the first time when I was six years old. I didn't know what I was looking at, but the group of boys with the haphazardly ripped-out magazine page said it was sex. Not long after came the full magazines with completely naked women. A few years later came dial-up Internet and online videos.

I remember when I got caught the first time. Mom learned how to search the browser history. I heard a scream come from the computer room and then hard, fast steps coming across the house. She asked what I'd been doing on the computer, and I tried to act like I didn't know what she was talking about, but the guilt was written all over my face. When Dad got home from work, we had a long discussion about how porn objectifies and degrades women and how it's filthy and shameful. We talked about how it's a sin and abhorrent to God.

Instead of an about-face, I got better at covering my tracks. I tried to justify to myself, and eventually my wife, that it was normal. But I never could get past the feeling of shame and filth. Finally, after several difficult conversations, Brittani's opposition struck a responsive cord, and I made the conscious decision to no longer indulge in pornography of any kind. The urge was still there. The temptation was *everywhere*. But I made a choice to always choose my bride over lustful fantasy.

Great. Story's over, right? I deny myself the urge to watch porn, and we all lived happily ever after? Nope. True, I quit watching porn, which was a victory in itself, but I didn't think it was necessary to stop masturbating. We all need a release every once in a while, right? I mean, the "sex doctors" on TV all tell us it's ok as long as it's not obsessive. I just had a very active libido, and I didn't want to *burden* my wife with constant sexual contact. I was really doing her a favor.

Oh, brother.

I could come up with *any* excuse for justification. Although I tried to convince myself that masturbating was a normal, healthy activity, the same feelings of shame and filthiness would come back time and time again.

I wanted to stop.

What bothered me most was that I didn't seem to have enough self-control to *deny myself* the desire for instant sexual gratification.

Are we really free if we can't be free of our own vices?

I knew I didn't want to do it anymore, but the urge was just too strong. Or I was just too weak. And I had learned my lesson with my wife from the pornography discussions: sell harder. I actually convinced my wife that it was absolutely impossible for me to abstain from masturbating.

So what happened? How did I decide I could actually survive without playing pocket pool?

What I craved more than anything was *freedom*. Sexual impurity was my master, and I was its slave. But I realized that I could control what thoughts I allowed to permeate my mind by limiting what I viewed or read. If I could stop the impure thoughts before they went too far, I at least stood a chance. Controlling those thoughts wouldn't be easy, and training my mind to reject inappropriate sexual thought impulses would be a mammoth undertaking, but I decided that this battle was mine to win.

• • •

Playing the Game

> I am the master of my fate, I am the captain of my soul. (From *Invictus* by William Ernest Henley)

As of the time of publication, I'm thirty-six years old. It's been over eight years since I've masturbated, and, if it's not obvious already, I'm still alive. Actually, it's like I've been given a new life—a better one. My sex life is amazing, and although I still want it more often than my wife does (I'm sure you can relate, guys), it's more frequent, it's fulfilling, and it's fireworks.

I had some startling realizations, and by listening to what God was calling me to do (or *not* do), I made the hard but necessary decision to completely refrain from pleasuring myself sexually. What's interesting is that I had this epiphany four years before finding *Every Man's Battle* by Stephen Arterburn and Fred Stoeker. If you or someone you know is struggling with any type of sexual addiction, I cannot overstate the importance of their book. Get a copy now!

Everything Arterburn and Stoeker discussed in their book was exactly what I had felt. I appreciate their realness and courage to tell it like it is. The book offers a healthy dose of tough love, so lock into the "coachability" mindset, and take a deep breath.

The following passage is especially convicting:

We aren't victims of some vast conspiracy to ensnare us sexually; we've simply chosen to mix in our own standards of sexual conduct with God's standard. Since we found God's standard too difficult, we created a mixture—something new, something comfortable, something mediocre... God's standard is that we avoid every hint of sexual immorality in our lives.

Abstaining from physical adultery, strip clubs, masturbation, and so on is great, but just how exclusive does God want us to be? Matthew 5:28 states, "But I tell you that anyone who looks at a woman lustfully has already committed adultery with her in his heart" (NIV). I've always found this passage difficult to digest. I mean, even *looking* at a woman lustfully is considered adultery? Really, has anyone other than Jesus ever not violated this commandment? The times I've looked at a woman lustfully are immeasurable. Saying it's difficult to see a beautiful woman and not think sexual thoughts would be an understatement, for me, anyway. But I also believe in a God that forgives and that we can repent of our sins and change our sinful nature. It's a choice—a hard one but, still, a choice.

You can't stop a bird from landing on your head, but you can stop him from building a nest. (Martin Luther)

Arterburn and Stoeker suggest conditioning yourself to avoid lustful thoughts by "bouncing your eyes." Whenever you see something that may cause you to stumble lustfully, simply look in a different direction. I use the word "simply," but looking in a different direction when a busty blonde bombshell wants to show off the goods isn't exactly simple, is it? Bouncing my eyes has been a difficult skill to learn, especially when society says it's no big deal.

Think about your circle of friends. What are the topics most often discussed? In some of my previous circles, it was always work, women, and sports and in that order. How do you change from a lustful hound dog to a respectful gentleman when everything and everyone around says it's no big deal? Do you even want to change?

Let me tell you from the experience of my own trials and failures: it's worth all the effort, pain, and struggle. You have to *hate* your impurity. You won't get it at first. It will take time, courage, persistence, and mostly prayer. But through persistence, you'll develop the grit and tenacity necessary to win the battle. You'll wonder why you waited so long to fight. It's worth it, my friend. You can do this.

Drugs and Alcohol

Sexual self-gratification isn't the only form of self-denial we need to focus on, although it may be the most important.

Here's another unpopular opinion: give up the alcohol.

Is there something evil about alcohol in and of itself? No. Jesus turned water into wine, remember? Did He do this so His friends at the wedding banquet could get blitzed? Absolutely not. It's a narrative about His first miracle and about cultural honor, not drinking. Typically, Jewish wedding banquet hosts would serve the best wine first and then, after the guests had their senses dulled, bring out the cheap stuff. The hosts didn't even have the cheap stuff left. More people showed up to the party than they had expected, and they were run dry.

Jesus was asked by His mother Mary to keep the hosts from being dishonored and shamed. Jesus not only provided more wine but also provided the highest of quality that so impressed the master of the banquet he pulled the bridegroom aside to express his amazement of the honor of the hosts to serve even better wine after the good stuff was gone.

I've sold life insurance for a large portion of my career. I won't get into my opinions of which type of policy is best, but I will point out something very interesting: Underwriters considering new applicants are very interested in how many drinks you have per week. Statistics point to significant reduction in life expectancy for those who consume too much alcohol.

I once submitted an application for a client and pre-screened her for the normal issues like diabetes, cancer, blood pressure, and build, but I received a declination notice from the insurance company a few days later that had me floored. This young woman was healthy and active, so why in the world was she declined?

When I called the underwriter for an explanation, they stated that she told them in her phone interview that she drinks twenty-four to thirty beers per week. They didn't offer the policy at a higher rate, or a lower death benefit. They flat denied her coverage because she drinks too much, according to the statistics.

Think about those amounts for a second. On average, she consumes about four beers per day. If you drink, you may be thinking, *That's not very much, really*. I only recently gave up alcohol, and before I did, I would average around ten drinks per week. I felt like I was a very light drinker. Many would agree, but the potential negative effects, even at this level, are concerning:

1. Inflammation
2. High blood pressure
3. Liver cancer

4. Stroke
5. Pancreatitis

Apart from the negative health consequences, I also chose not to drink for the following reasons:

1. To save money
2. To feel better
3. To obey God's calling for me

The Bible doesn't tell us that drinking alcohol is a sin. The Bible does tell us that drunkenness is a sin. I don't think God is calling everyone to completely refrain from consuming alcohol, but if something in you feels like you should, please know you're not alone. I'm truly surprised at how many people I talk to that don't drink at all.

> Do not get drunk with wine, which leads to debauchery. Instead, be filled with the Spirit... (Ephesians 5:18 NIV)

> ...for drunkards and gluttons become poor, and drowsiness clothes them in rags. (Proverbs 23:21 NIV)

To be fair, there are also scriptures that seem to accept alcohol, and even Jesus drank wine:

> The Son of Man came eating and drinking, and they say, "Here is a glutton and a drunkard, a friend of tax collectors and sinners." But wisdom is proved right by her deeds. (Matthew 11:19 NIV)

In this scripture, Jesus was pointing out that critics were contradicting themselves. They claimed that John the Baptist's avoidance of eating and drinking was caused by a demon but then accused Jesus of being a "glutton and a drunkard" because He ate and drank with tax collectors and sinners.

Did you notice the last sentence of that scripture? "But wisdom is proved right by her deeds." What does that mean? Jesus and John the Baptist both had wisdom that was evidenced by the outcomes of their actions. Although their methods differed, what mattered was the genuine content of their lessons.

I don't have experience with drugs, so I won't write much on that. I think it's self-evident that substance abuse in any fashion is dangerous and harmful to more than just the user. However, I would like to point out that drug addiction is a very powerful and difficult thing to overcome. Drug addicts don't need condescension; they need hope.

If you or someone you know is struggling, please seek help. There are people that genuinely care, people that have walked the same path, and people that want to see you succeed that can help you get out.

Phone Usage

We're living in an interesting time. Technology has advanced at an exponential rate and will continue to do so faster and faster. New artificial intelligence is doing some amazing (sometimes *scary*) things. But being continuously plugged in to the digital world causes some serious problems.

Our phones do almost everything for us now. But having all of that power in the palm of our hand makes it incredibly easy to become distracted.

Here are some alarming facts about phone usage:

1. Thirty-eight percent of people routinely check *e-mail* at the dinner table.
2. Sixty-nine percent of people cannot go to sleep without checking their inbox.
3. Seventy-five percent of people *admit* to using their phone in the bathroom.

Think about these stats for a minute. Do any of them apply to you? How would you feel if you were boarding a plane for vacation and realized you left your phone at home? Would you be able to enjoy your vacation without the distractions, or would you be stressed about what you might be missing or who may need to contact you?

Try a day without any electronics. Get outside and do something active. Play basketball with your kids, go on a long walk or run, do some landscaping, go hunting or fishing, plant a garden, play golf, go mountain biking. Just do something without distraction.

How do we begin to deny ourselves? By prioritizing others. We shift the focus from our own shortcomings to the needs of others. We shift the focus from our sins and guilt to our loved ones and the life we want for them. We shift the focus from the shame we feel to the knowledge that everyone struggles with something. We have the power to choose to make a covenant with ourselves to think about the well-being of others before giving in to our own selfish temptations.

In order to accept this challenge, however, you must have a firm knowledge of yourself. The Greek phrase "know thyself" is attributed to Socrates and has inspired a multitude of philosophical texts. When we seek to understand who we are and truly know ourselves, we begin to unlock the secrets to finding our identity.

Self-Denial

Maybe your conscience speaks to you differently. I realize this topic is confrontational and people will strongly disagree. That's ok. I do have one request, though: be honest with yourself. Don't just chalk it up to "everyone else does it." Listen to that still, small voice deep within you, and have the courage to deny yourself the things that separate you from your Creator.

In his book, *The War of Art*, Steven Pressfield describes our struggle to accomplish a worthy goal or overcome an addiction as "Resistance" with a capital "R." It's a faceless enemy that wages war on each of us in a multitude of cunning methods. We are typically keen to the effects of Resistance when we begin to make progress. It can cause us to procrastinate indefinitely, come up with elaborate justifications for avoiding completion of the goal, and so on. Pressfield warns "any act that rejects immediate gratification in favor of long-term growth, health, or integrity [elicits Resistance]."

Forgiving Yourself vs. Not Giving a Crap

In order to move on from past hurts, we must forgive. When we've been the problem that caused the hurt, we have to forgive ourselves, which can oftentimes be more difficult than forgiving others.

There are people that choose to go through life not giving a crap, who ignore the negative effects of their words and actions on those around them. People that buy into the notion that not giving a crap can make you happy are missing something important: humans are communal beings. There is a big difference between the contentment felt when you forgive yourself and the conceit of not caring.

When you forgive yourself, you develop a new paradigm. You're able to look at the world through new lenses and realize that God meant for you to be happy. You can rest with the knowledge of understanding you're human and therefore not perfect. Forgiving yourself is acknowledging your faults and mistakes, repenting and moving forward, and accepting that you can't change the past but you can choose to be a better person from this moment forward. Forgiving yourself gives you a peace that surpasses the worry of others' judgment. You're not worried about what other people think because you know who you are and *whose* you are.

People that have forgiven themselves and know themselves are often mistaken for people who just don't give a crap because of their easy-going nature. The difference is their inner being, which is expressed in the way they treat others.

Not giving a crap is saying, "I am who I am and I don't need to change. Who are you to judge me? Only God can judge me." You can recognize these people quickly and easily. They're typically loud and obnoxious and treat others like garbage. They post vague, passive-aggressive, attention-seeking comments on social media about other people. They yell obscenities in a crowd of people, regardless of who may be listening. They're often self-proclaimed a-holes like it's something to be proud of. They're bullies. Here's the secret about folks that "don't give a crap": they're the loneliest, most insecure people you know. Yes, your parents were exactly right when they told you the mean kid at school acted that way because he doesn't like himself.

Self-Control

Denying yourself, in many ways, is simply having self-control. We tend to think of refraining from overeating as the go-to example of possessing self-control. Proverbs 25:27–28 says, "It is not good to eat much honey, or to seek honor on top of honor. Like a city breached, without walls, is one who lacks self-control" (NRSV).

When we indulge too often in pleasure, we lose track of what's truly important. Pleasure (or amusement) doesn't help us grow. It doesn't challenge us. It allows us to escape from discomfort temporarily. Discomfort doesn't mean we need to get out of the current situation. Discomfort means we're in unfamiliar territory and, if we're paying attention, growing and learning. Embracing the discomfort and navigating through it causes massive growth.

C.S. Lewis writes the following on self-control in his book *Mere Christianity*:

> A man who makes his golf or his motor-bicycle the centre of his life, or a woman who devotes all her thoughts to clothes or bridge or her dog, is being just as "intemperate" as someone who gets drunk every evening. Of course, it does not show on the outside so easily; bridge-mania or golf-mania do not make you fall down in the middle of the road. But God is not deceived by externals.

So, possessing strong self-control means avoiding all the fun stuff, right? Actually, not at all. Fun and play are important for everyone, even adults. As long as the fun is a morally sound activity, it's actually good for your health and happiness to do the things you enjoy. Self-control isn't about restricting fun; it's recognizing the proper balance of work and play, education and entertainment, and productivity and leisure.

How much time do you spend watching TV or scrolling Facebook, Twitter, Instagram, and so on? How often do you feel completely stuffed after a meal? How often do you go shopping or log into Amazon and buy things that aren't necessities? How often do you go to the casino or buy scratchers and lottery tickets? Self-control isn't about avoiding these things altogether. Self-control is about understanding that too much of any of them can have disastrous consequences on our physical, mental, spiritual, and financial health.

When we've established a clear understanding of what self-control means to us individually, we free ourselves from the bondage of the consequences of overindulgence. Self-control allows us to find the contentment necessary for true happiness.

Self-Discipline and Integrity

> The man that masters himself through self-discipline can never be mastered by others. (Napoleon Hill)

Discipline is the ability to give myself a command and then follow it. How many times have we told ourselves, "I'm going to drop 10 pounds by eating healthy and exercising thirty minutes every day" and then failed to follow through after a couple weeks? How often do we create a task list and then find something else less relevant or important to focus on? Discipline isn't about creating a comfortable routine and occasionally doing something difficult. Discipline is holding yourself to a higher standard of acceptable behavior and consistently following through with what you say you will do, whether or not anyone else knows about the commitment.

Discipline is very closely related to integrity. While discipline is about your actions, integrity is about your morality. My parents hung a poster above the stairwell in my childhood home. I saw that poster every day when I walked downstairs for breakfast. It read, "Stand up for what is right, even if you're standing alone." That's integrity.

Your moral compass will lead you down a lonely path occasionally, but it will never steer you wrong. You may hear about how hard it is to find real, honest people in this "day and age," but you'll be surprised how many will be walking beside you when you decide to take the high road. It may not be the immediate group of friends you're with right now, and that's ok. The real world isn't as dark as news and social media outlets make it out to be.

When you live with integrity, you attract other people of integrity to you. Integrity is about complete honesty and transparency. It's about understanding your moral principles and never compromising them. Whether you work in sales, construction, health and human services, manufacturing, or whatever your occupation, integrity makes you stand out because others aren't willing to be that honest. It makes them feel vulnerable. They think they stand to lose everything or that they'll be found out and labeled a fraud or that they'll lose ground compared to their peers and the competition.

Here's the truth: everyone makes mistakes, and people actually understand when you fess up about it and trust you *more*. Now, I'm not saying you can just keep screwing up and people will keep giving you more chances. And, yes, some people will write you off after the first offense. But don't worry about the people who are unforgiving and vindictive. They're typically not the people you want to associate with anyway. What I am saying is that integrity will give you peace of mind that comes from knowing that even if you lose out on short-term gain, your reputation of being trustworthy will remain intact and lead to bigger and better opportunities down the road. The falsity we hear so often is that if we don't close the deal by whatever means necessary, the opportunity will never present itself again. The truth is that avoiding dishonesty and choosing to do what's right, even if no one else is, will lead to greater gain.

Here's another interesting tidbit about integrity. In his book *The Millionaire Next Door*, Thomas J. Stanley states that through extensive research, he found that the vast majority of millionaires have levels of integrity that are off the charts. While most people feel like they're "pretty

Playing the Game

honest people," millionaires possess almost fanatical levels of integrity. Millionaires refuse to compromise their moral principles in any circumstance. Makes you wonder, doesn't it? Maybe the next time you're faced with a moral dilemma, this information could influence your decision.

CHAPTER 8

COMPETITION, COMPARISON, AND COMMON SENSE

Competition

Sports and competition are synonymous. One team pitted against another on the gridiron, one individual battling another in a wrestling match, us versus them, me versus you, winners and losers.

You must get over the thought that taking action doesn't matter just because you won't be the best. Even the best aren't the best all the time, but they have learned that doing something is far better than doing nothing. Take action because it will move you one peg closer to your goal. Take action because it will change your view.

Playing the Game

Each peg allows you to see a little more and to see things in a different light.

Sometimes the action we take will cause us to fall a couple pegs. That's ok! It's never fun to lose ground, but *moving* is what's important. You will have gained valuable insight from that misstep and be able to use it to gain sure footing in the future.

Here's the thing about the pegs: you never reach the last one. But wouldn't it be terrible to not be able to grow anymore? We tend to think that when we set out for a goal that we'll reach the end, that we'll finally be able to rest after we've hustled so hard for so long, but life isn't about finishing. Life is about doing. Life is about action. Life is about living and experiencing a progressive realization of worthy ideals! In fact, that is my favorite definition of success. Here it is again: a progressive realization of a worthy ideal.

Success isn't something you can buy, or show, or hold. Success is the *process* of moving toward your goals, not necessarily reaching them. If your goal is to save $10 million by age 70 and you only make it to $8 million, are you a failure?

Reaching a goal gives us a sense of accomplishment and pride. But when we've reached that "pinnacle," we relish the moment and move on. If we decide to get comfortable and relax, we begin moving backwards. But what happens when we're exhausted? What happens when we feel like we've gone far enough?

We think, *This is ok. I don't need to keep climbing these pegs. All my friends are here, and it's cozy. If I keep climbing, I'll always be tired and lonely. I'll just stay put.*

Improving ourselves is difficult. It takes effort and significant investments of time and, sometimes, money. Others will question you, doubt you, belittle you, and even berate you, but that's where your vision and clarity come in. If you have a strong vision of where you're going, you know that the climb is worth the criticism.

My first job after college was with a leading car rental company. I interviewed with four different people to get the job, and the common question for each meeting was, "Are you competitive?"

It was a sales position with a management training label. The first week was a whirlwind of orientation and sales training. I was promptly introduced to the sales leaderboard that tracked the total sales of each frontline employee across the Kansas City region. The ultimate goal was to be at the top of this list. It meant parties with the regional directors and managers, faster promotions, name recognition, and so on. Needless to say, a few employees "bent" the rules and tossed ethics aside when it came to vying for a top spot. They always got caught. Sometimes they were reprimanded. Sometimes they were unofficially encouraged. I legitimately earned a spot on the leaderboard twice during my one-year stint with the company, and it felt good. Even being underpaid and overworked, the job still had its perks. I met some great people and learned some incredibly valuable business and life lessons there.

Competition has driven the American economic engine for generations. The problem with the world's view of competition is that we tend to take an unhealthy view of how to "get ahead." When we compromise our integrity to climb the ladder, it will always result in consequences. The timing and severity will vary, but it's never worth it. As individuals, we need to shift our focus to what competition really is: it's being better than the person I was yesterday.

Chris Nikic, along with his Unified Partner Dan Grieb, was the first person with Down syndrome to finish an Ironman and has a beautiful take on self-competition: He says, "I try to be 1% better than I was yesterday. In a year, that's a 365% improvement!"

Comparison

Unhealthy competition with others pits us in a dangerous game of comparisons. The summer after my eighth grade year, our football coach started us on the Bigger, Faster, Stronger program in the weight room. It was a weightlifting and conditioning program designed specifically for high school football athletes. As a 5'6", 100-pound (soaking wet) eighth grader, this was very appealing. I didn't miss any workouts over the summer, and I had started to grow and had gotten much stronger. What I lacked in size, I made up for in speed. Still, I compared my size to some of my peers and kids my age from other schools and thought it just wasn't working for me. I had forgotten to look at the progress I had made over the summer. I made a comment to one of my coaches about being small, and he said, "Ben, you're a freshman, and a late bloomer. You've come a long way from the beginning of summer. If you stick with the weights and conditioning and really do your best every day, it will all come together eventually."

I took his words to heart. He didn't have to tell me to stop comparing myself to others. He simply shifted my focus to what I could control: showing up and doing my best, every day.

You may have heard the quote "comparison is the thief of joy," and that is certainly true. When we compare our bodies, our abilities, our experiences, our lifestyle, our material possessions, and anything else to that of others, we lose sight of blessings God has given us. In the next chapter, we'll discuss contentment.

Common Sense

We regularly hear this phrase. And when we hear it, we know we have it because it's always about other people who seem to lack it. It seems to be something you either have or don't have, not one particular piece of knowledge or another. It contains a certain connotation of intelligence. But what is common sense, really? To be honest, I have always had the idea that common sense must be something people are born with, something that is innately imbedded within our DNA. If we don't have it, there's no chance of getting it and we're doomed to stay stupid forever. Those poor ignorant souls seemed to congregate in groups, and if one of them lacked it, their parents, children, siblings, and close friends probably did as well. But here's the kicker: common sense *is* directly dependent on the group you *common*ly congregate with. But it's not whether you're intelligent or not. It's whether or not you share similar perspectives and life experiences.

A few synonyms for "sense" are *feeling, idea,* and *purpose*. Think about that for a minute. Those words have nothing to do with *truth, realities, statistics,* or *data,* which are synonyms for "facts." Isn't that the idea we have when we hear the phrase "common sense"? My thoughts used to be, *These people should know these facts about this particular thing. Do they not have any common sense?* Just like when a virus is ultimately rendered obsolete via herd immunity, ignorance is erased when the group is introduced to a new idea and it is shared and discussed.

CHAPTER 9

HAPPINESS

> Happy is a man who finds wisdom and who acquires understanding, for she is more profitable than silver, and her revenue is better than gold. She is more precious than jewels; nothing you desire can equal her. Long life is in her right hand; in her left, riches and honor. Her ways are pleasant and all her paths, peaceful. She is a tree of life to those who embrace her, and those who hold on to her are happy. (Proverbs 3:13–18 CSB)

What Is Happiness?

What is *real* happiness? Occasionally, we have experiences that make us wish we could live in that moment forever. But is that really what being happy is all about? Is happiness simply moments of fleeting bliss, or is there hope for more consistency?

Think of someone you know who seems to always be happy. You probably pictured someone that is always smiling and cheerful, right? We tend to believe that happiness is a state of cheerfulness, elation, or ecstasy, which is absolutely false. Think of Will Smith's character Chris Gardner in *The Pursuit of Happyness* after he's offered his dream job and walks out of the glass high-rise onto a crowded sidewalk barely able to contain his excitement. His narrative voice over says, "This part of my life... This part right here? This is called happiness."

Although it's a beautiful cinematic moment (the climax of the movie plot), it's an inaccurate description of real happiness. In that moment, he's completely euphoric. I won't argue that euphoria doesn't include happiness because it does. But I will argue that you can be happy without constant euphoria. We get these false messages over and over and believe that we have to be inundated with euphoria in order to consider ourselves "happy." Happiness is simply a choice rather than the result of our circumstances. We can choose to be grateful for what we have, and as long as we have breath in our lungs, we have *something*. From gratitude, we learn contentment, and from contentment, we achieve happiness.

Gratitude → contentment → happiness

Gratitude

Gratitude makes sense of our past, brings peace for today, and creates vision for tomorrow. (Zig Ziglar)

Are you thankful because you're happy, or are you happy because you're thankful? I would argue the latter, although it's much easier to be thankful when we're feeling "happy." Thankfulness isn't about waiting until you can sit back once you've "arrived" and take an inventory of everything you have. Thankfulness is about consciously thinking or praying about the things we've been blessed with like food, shelter, clothing, health, family, friends, and the fact that we're still breathing.

What about trials? Difficult individuals or situations? Bad days, financial hardships, sickness, last-minute change of plans, or an argument with your best friend? Are we thankful for those? Should we be? 1 Thessalonians 5:16–18 says, "Rejoice always, pray continually, give thanks in all circumstances; for this is God's will for you in Christ Jesus."

I won't try to sugarcoat the hard times. Sometimes, moments in life get too hard to really be happy. When we lose loved ones, lose a job, become ill, or just seem to be stuck in a rut, it's pretty hard, maybe seemingly impossible to consider ourselves happy. But happiness is more than living in the moment. Happiness is about your overall state of mind regarding your life and the direction you're headed.

Victory

Happiness isn't found in pleasure. We don't become happier as we experience more pleasure. We become happy through victory, mostly over ourselves. Victory isn't just setting a goal and completing it. Victory is in each step you take toward your goals. Victory is letting go of our fears and moving forward. Victory is hiding in the failures that inevitably take place while you're working toward those goals because each failure offers the opportunity to learn something.

One of my favorite old hymns is "Victory in Jesus" by E M Bartlett. The second verse is my favorite:

> *I heard about His healing*
> *Of His cleansing power revealing*
> *How He made the lame to walk again*
> *And caused the blind to see*
> *And then I cried, "Dear Jesus, come and heal my broken spirit"*
> *And somehow Jesus came and brought to me the victory*

The true victory (true happiness) lies with Jesus. He's already won the battle. He was victorious over sin, and we have been forgiven.

Giving/Service

Happiness begins where selfishness ends. (John Wooden)

How do we find lasting, consistent happiness? One piece of the puzzle is to be a generous giver. But what should we give away, and how much? I'm sure you've heard someone say you should give your time, talents, and resources in some capacity. But is there a specific way you should give? Is one category more important than the others?

The easiest, and yet sometimes the most difficult, form of giving is money. It doesn't require your most sacred resource (time), and it doesn't require you to possess or acquire any specific talents. Studies have shown that people who give away 10% of their income are much happier and content with what they already have. You may have heard the word "tithing" if you were raised in a Christian household. The word "tithe" literally means 1/10th.

When I was about six, I wondered why God needed my $1 bill and what difference such a small amount of money could actually make. When I was ten, I thought tithing was a ploy enacted by the church to make sure the doors would stay open. When I started earning my own money in my teens, I would put $20 in the offering plate, occasionally. And the amounts and frequency hardly changed through my mid-twenties. It wasn't until twenty-seven that I listened well enough to learn that tithing isn't about making sure God got His cut or about the church "staying in business." Tithing is about *perspective.*

It seems illogical to give away some of our possessions, especially when we're already struggling financially. When you work through your budget and see that large number, you think, *I could use that for so many things right now.* But giving away 10% of your income isn't logical; it's *psychological.* Whether you're a Christian or not, giving away a portion of your income has major psychological benefits.

Feeling good about giving is an obvious by-product, but is it why we should be giving in the first place? I know the virtuous and honorable answer is, "No, we should give without any expectation of return." But seriously, any expectation of return would include the good feeling because, really, that's priceless. If I'm supposed to give without *any* expectation of return, wouldn't that include the good feeling? That's a hard question and require even harder answer.

I believe God created us to be givers. Showing love by offering something that cannot be returned is the selfless love we're called to bestow upon one another. But I also believe God created us to be receivers. The catch is (pun intended), we can't have one without the other.

Dave Ramsey created a great visual: Think of your hand wrapped around a hundred dollars. If it's a closed fist, no one can take it from you; however, you can't receive anything either. When you open your hand, some will need what you have, which you offer freely. Others, however, see your open hand and offer you some of what they have. In the end, you'll end up with more than you had before.

Don't get tied up on monetary giving, though. Giving of your time is a common conception as well, but don't forget about giving your love, kindness, affection, talents, knowledge, experience, and the list goes on. Sometimes it's more difficult to receive some of these than it is to give them. Am I right? Maybe we don't feel like we deserve them, or maybe we think they need to be reserved for those who need them more than we do. If you listen to anything I say in this book, listen to this: it is crucially important for you to accept love, kindness, affection, help, experience, money, compliments, and time from a trusted source.

We tend to "politely" decline the offer from the giver for many reasons, but the truth is, we're denying them the opportunity to give. Yes, giving is an opportunity.

Whether you feel you're worthy of the gift or not, it's not ours to deny. Receiving these gifts is as much a part of the giving process as dropping a $20 in the offering plate at church. I get it—you don't want to feel like you're a charity case. I've been there. I've felt guilty about accepting anything from anyone for many different reasons. The fact is, we need to become comfortable with acknowledging and accepting what is freely offered to us.

Often, the feeling we get from the gift we gave is more of a reward than anything materialistic. I'm sure you've been there. Maybe you sat with a friend for a couple hours who was going through a really hard time and just listened to them. Maybe you offered some heartfelt advice. You didn't miss the time or kindness you gave them. In fact, you probably felt better after that conversation, too. What selfless giving boils down to is love—real love.

When we become happy, obligations become opportunities. We often find ourselves over-extended with commitments that can easily cause resentment and irritation. For example, remember when you volunteered for the PTO fundraiser brainstorming session two months ago? It's tomorrow, and you have a hundred other things way more important things to do than deciding between selling frozen burritos or cheap chocolate, *but* you promised you'd help, so your character and integrity won't let you skip.

When you're happy, your perspective changes. You're not irritated about having to show up to the meeting; you see the opportunities that lie within. Maybe you're in sales and this is your forte. Your knowledge and experience could make this fundraiser so successful that it will generate enough profit that the group won't have to do any more fundraisers the rest of the year. Maybe you have a friend serving on PTO with you that you haven't gotten to visit with in quite a while. Maybe you've seen how other groups have had great success and have some ideas on how to improve the overall function of the club.

We all do things that we seem to force ourselves to get through grudgingly, but when we actually look for the golden nuggets of opportunity within each situation, we find them more often than not.

Do you list happiness as a goal? Is one of your New Year's resolutions to "be a happier person"? Should happiness be a goal? I used to think so. Rick Warren thinks otherwise. He says, "Making happiness your goal in life will always have the opposite effect. Happiness comes from right thinking, right living, and right acting. It's the by-product—but never, ever the goal." Rick is saying true happiness comes from living a righteous life. Happiness itself isn't something we should be working toward; instead, we should be focused on being like Jesus. Once we've decided to live our lives according to Jesus' teachings, we are immersed in happiness.

People of the highest integrity are often the happiest among us. Why? They have nothing to hide, and they're content with themselves. People of integrity live their lives with an unbreakable moral code and tend to be others-centric. They don't think about themselves and their problems; rather, they think about others and how they can help them. Believe it or not, when you take the focus off of yourself, you tend to think less about your problems and shortcomings leaving more room for thought about others. When you think about others, you think about their happiness in one way or another.

The Rollercoaster

The truth about happiness is that we have to experience lows to appreciate the highs. Life happens. Loved ones die, people disappoint or even betray you, natural disasters occur, and accidents happen that can have major consequences. We can't be happy in perpetuity.

The key to getting through the lows is hope. As bleak as circumstances may seem, there is always hope. In the end, we have the hope of eternal salvation through our Lord Jesus Christ.

"For I know the plans I have for you," declares the Lord, "plans to prosper you and not to harm you, plans to give you hope and a future." (Jeremiah 29:11 NIV)

God wants us to be happy. He wants you to prosper. For most of us, our unhappiness is our own doing by putting our hope and trust in imperfect humans, but we can reverse course. We can place our trust in our Heavenly Father and seek His ways and trust in His provision. When we're in the rut and frustrated with our inability to get out on our own, we learn to turn to Him. Our temporary unhappiness is a valuable opportunity to acquire understanding and grow closer to God.

The perspective of happiness is relative. Remember the discussion about paradigms? We all view happiness a little differently, according to our experiences and environment. More often than not, we don't think we're happy because we're too busy thinking about what we don't have. Stop that.

Our church takes a bi-annual trip to Juarez, Mexico, to build houses for people that can't afford them. Locals generally make about $50–70 per week, which barely covers the cost to feed their families. The build sites are actually in Anapra, which is literally built upon the old garbage dump site of Juarez. People build their home with whatever they can find, usually old pallets and tarps. Garbage lines the streets, and sewage runs down the roads for lack of modern plumbing.

What completely floored me the first time going on the trip was the children. The people were generally very clean despite the environment, but the children were also joyful and playful, even the older ones. Their circumstances were dreadful (according to our American standards), but they didn't seem to notice. They weren't focused on what they didn't have. They were too busy playing games with one another and being entertained by our humorous antics. By the way, if you have kids, you already know bubbles are an international sensation. It doesn't matter where you're from; if you're under ten years old, bubbles are magical. We gave them several bottles of bubbles, and you would have thought we gave the children new iPhones the way their faces lit up.

Some of the happiest people on the planet are those that have the least (materially speaking). Why is that? One could make an argument that ignorance is bliss, and I get that, but the people in Anapra can see across the fence all of the shiny objects in "the land of opportunity" yet they still don't dwell on what they can't quite touch. Happiness is a mindset, a choice to continually refocus on gratitude and contentment, focusing on what we have, not what we don't. Happiness is receiving life like a child.

Coincidentally (or not), Jesus tells us that's how we must receive the kingdom of God:

> But Jesus called the children to him and said, "Let the little children come to me, and do not hinder them, for the kingdom of God belongs to such as these. Truly I tell you, anyone who will not receive the kingdom of God like a little child will never enter it." (Luke 18:16–17 NIV)

Joy Over Happiness

One last thought on happiness:

I recognize our worldview of happiness is not something we can maintain in perpetuity, but joy is. What I've described in this chapter on happiness is a buildup to what God calls us to focus on instead of happiness itself.

What's the difference between happiness and joy?

Happiness is an emotion ranging from contentment and satisfaction to bliss or intense pleasure. Joy is a lasting emotion that comes from the choice to trust that God will fulfill his promises.

> Consider it pure joy, brothers and sisters, whenever you face trials of many kinds, because you know that the testing of your faith produces

perseverance. Let perseverance finish its work so that you may be mature and complete, not lacking anything. If any of you lacks wisdom, you should ask God, who gives generously to all without finding fault, and it will be given to you. But when you ask, you must believe and not doubt, because the one who doubts is like a wave of the sea, blown and tossed by the wind. That person should not expect to receive anything from the Lord. Such a person is double-minded and unstable in all they do. (James 1:2–8 NIV)

CHAPTER 10
===

Our Relationship with God

Jesus looked at them and said, "With man this is impossible, but not with God; all things are possible with God." (Mark 10:27 NIV)

Faithfulness

It seems like society's message to Christians today is, "Fine. Keep your faith, but keep it quiet and keep it to yourself." Society marginalizes God. Society wants us to believe that God is down the list of importance somewhere between major holidays and family reunions. Society wants us to believe that our jobs, politics, bank accounts, and social media following are all more important than our relationship with God.

Playing the Game

    I like to think of myself as an educated, logical individual. I consider various perspectives or opinions before making a decision on important issues, but I hold fast to a set of morals and values that I cannot contradict. When it comes to the issue of faith, especially Christianity, it can be easy to have doubts when you try to look at it from a logical standpoint, especially when we can't see, hear, or touch what we believe is real. Faith and hope in something intangible isn't logical. It's a choice to confidently pursue a deeper understanding of something that cannot be scientifically confirmed. Christian faith often conflicts with conventional wisdom. I mean, walking on water, turning water into wine, and rising from the dead after three days in a tomb aren't easily explained from a logical point of view, right?

    The truths that you learn on your own (maybe with some guidance), instead of the ones you're told, are the most powerful. For example, for me, it was learning that my needs, desires, and worries in this world are nothing when I finally chose to fully accept God's promise. What He has prepared for me in Heaven is unimaginably greater than anything on Earth, and whatever struggle I face is unbelievably short-lived when compared with the eternal fulfillment of Heaven. I'm sure I've heard it 1,000 times from Sunday school, Vacation Bible School, church sermons, Christian music, and the list goes on. But I never really let it sink in until 2015.

I don't remember the exact day, but it was late spring, and I needed to mow the lawn. I grabbed my earbuds and phone like usual, but instead of running through the familiar music playlist, I decided to listen to some Zig Ziglar speeches.

My wife and I had recently "graduated" from Dave Ramsey's Financial Peace University, and Dave had used several of Zig's quotes throughout the program. I had never heard of him before FPU, but I thought, *If Dave Ramsey is quoting Zig Ziglar this much, he must be a big deal.*

Immediately, I was drawn in by Zig's smooth, Southern twang and confident, bold speaking. He reminded me of my Uncle Steve, a fearless Texan teacher and preacher with a smile as big as Texas and a handshake that would break every bone in your hand if you didn't give it the same enthusiasm.

I originally opted for Zig for his lessons on personal development and how to be successful, but what I discovered after the first ten minutes of listening was convicting, to say the least.

For whatever reason, Zig's words hit me right in the feels, and tears began to flow as I slowly clipped along the yard on the rickety old John Deere. I realized my struggles didn't have to be just struggles. My own personal development and ultimate success were not only possible but highly probable. It was a choice I needed to make, as simple as that sounds. But I hadn't expected the foundation, the building blocks to success:

Faith and family

My focus had been all wrong.

Although it's easy to become bound up in our daily struggles, routines, and worries, it's important to remember that this world, this life, isn't our true home. However, it is an incredible gift, and God wants us to take full advantage of it and enjoy our time here. He also wants us to use our time here to learn more about Him and grow closer to Him before we're called home. Life is about *learning*. Life is about *growing* spiritually, physically, emotionally, and mentally.

Life is not about your past.

Life is not about your failures.

Life is not about missed opportunities.

But when analyzed through the correct lens, each of those things can help you learn and grow.

If you aren't aware, that lens is your relationship with Jesus Christ.

A Sinner's Guilt

We all feel the sting of guilt for our wrongdoings. Those with the highest levels of lifelong integrity tend to feel less guilt because they have nothing to hide, but none of us are without sin. I've sinned well beyond my fair share. At times, I've felt completely unconnected to God and undeserving of forgiveness. To be honest, I still do sometimes. No one deserves it, but God offers it freely anyway. Our "level" of sin is how we compare our wrongdoing against those of our peers and the "bad guys" we hear about in the news. The Bible tells us that sin is sin, regardless of severity. Nevertheless, we can't help but feel like we've failed when we mess up really bad.

1 Timothy 1:15-16 makes it clear how God feels about our past sins:

Here is a trustworthy saying that deserves full acceptance: Christ Jesus came into the world to save sinners-of whom I am the worst. But for that very reason I was shown mercy so that in me, the worst of sinners, Christ Jesus might display his immense patience as an example for those who would believe in him and receive eternal life. (NIV)

Understanding that God has already forgiven us was the biggest hurdle for me to clear. Once I fully accepted that Jesus' sacrifice really was to absolve me of my sins, all that was left was repentance. I once heard it said that there can be no forgiveness without repentance. I've thought about that often. What is repentance, really? And am I really not forgiven if I don't repent? *Webster* defines the root word "repent" as "to feel or express sincere regret or remorse about one's wrongdoing or sin." I've always taken it to mean *asking God for forgiveness for a specific wrongdoing*. But if He's already forgiven me, do I have to ask Him to forgive me again? I think the answer there is "no." Repentance is a feeling or expression of remorse, so if we don't have that feeling of remorse, there should be nothing of which we need forgiveness. But the definition also mentions *expressing* sincere regret. We need to prayerfully acknowledge our sins, and although we're already forgiven, I still ask for forgiveness because it helps me express to God my sincere remorse for having committed the sin.

As in all things with God, He doesn't need anything from us. We don't admit our failures and apologize because He needs us to. Acknowledging and apologizing for our sins is more about our hearts and the growth we gain from self-reflection and the freedom we feel from confession.

Providence

Some synonyms for providence are *fate, chance, luck,* and *destiny*. But the definition is something that honestly surprised me. Providence is defined as "the protective care of God or of nature as a spiritual power."

Everyone that's been a Christian for ten minutes has heard the story of Jesus and the loaves and fishes. Just a recap: Scriptures tell us that Jesus was preaching to a crowd of 5,000 men. They make no mention of the number of women and children, so historians and theologians estimate there were as many as 15,000 in attendance. When asked what they could feed the people, the disciples said it would take eight months' wages from each of them to feed the entire crowd. That's when the boy with five barley loaves and two small fishes is brought forward.

The disciple Andrew is the one who brings the boy forward. Witnessing what was basically the boy's lunch, Andrew asks, "How far will it go?" What he really means is, "We don't have much to work with here." But Jesus blesses the food, and it is distributed among the crowd. Not only does everyone eat their fill, but there are *twelve* baskets of food leftover! Miracles are God's way of showing us that He makes the impossible possible. God doesn't need much to work with to start a mighty story.

What's your story? Do you think it's insignificant? Do you ask yourself, "How far could I really go with the circumstances I'm stuck with? I don't have much to work with here." God doesn't need much to work with. He loves you more than you can imagine. Mother Teresa was one of the most amazing people to live since Jesus, and God loves you as much as He loves Mother Teresa. I don't know about you, but I can't quite comprehend that. His love for me is so great, He died on the cross for me so that I would be free from death and live with Him in Heaven for eternity if I only choose Him.

Perfectionism and WWJD

Perfectionists are playing an unwinnable game. I've been there and still struggle with it. So many people inaccurately assume, or subconsciously hold to the notion, that unless we achieve absolute perfection, we aren't truly successful. And success brings happiness, right? Not necessarily. Jesus was the only perfect human. But Jesus was fully God and fully man. None of us are God. However, we are taught in the church to live and love like Jesus. Kind of sets us perfectionists up for failure, doesn't it?

There's no way we can fully achieve the status of living and loving like Jesus because He was the one true perfect human. But He was also God. It also points to why many nonbelievers see Christians as hypocrites, and to be honest, they're not wrong. We are hypocrites, but not because we're trying to be. If we're truly Christians, we're striving to live as examples of God's grace: that despite our flaws and imperfections, He still loves us *even if we don't love Him back*. Maybe the point of trying to live and love like Jesus is the *struggle*. It's the growth we experience by struggling to overcome our weaknesses and flaws. In fact, 2 Corinthians 12:9 states the following:

> But he said to me, "My grace is sufficient for you, for my power is made perfect in weakness." Therefore I will boast all the more gladly about my weaknesses, so that Christ's power may rest on me. (NIV)

We may not be God, but God is within us. We just have to let go of our controlled perfectionist programming and allow Him to work.

Do I Need to Change to Follow Christ?

I saw a sermon about a conversation a pastor had with a kid who was wanting to follow Jesus but didn't want to give up smoking weed. The kid asks the pastor, "Do I need to give up pot in order to follow Jesus?"

Pastor says, "No."

Kid says, "No, I mean, do I need to give up *marijuana* to follow Jesus?"

"No."

"I don't think you understand." [pulls out a joint] "Do I need to give this up so that I can follow Jesus?"

"No."

"I don't understand."

"No, you don't understand. Think about it this way: do you need to get cleaned up to take a shower?"

"No, the shower cleans you up."

"It's the same with Jesus. You don't clean up your life to follow Jesus; you just decide to follow Him. By doing so, you will begin to see areas of your life that need to be cleaned up, and you'll work on that with Him."

Obviously, I'm not condoning drug use, but the point here is that so many people seem to think they can't decide to follow Jesus because they're not clean enough. Think back to 1 Timothy 1:15-16. Even the worst of sinners can come to the Father and be cleansed. The scripture doesn't say how long it takes because it's different for everyone. The point is to *decide* to accept His grace.

Truly, deeply, wholeheartedly following Jesus will change you in ways I can't explain because, honestly, I don't fully comprehend them. My life has changed immensely since I made the choice to submit my life to Him. It has taken me a long time to get where I am, but I didn't change in order to follow Christ. I began to follow Christ, and He continues to guide me and teach me the areas of my life and being that need to be changed.

In order to change, we must be obedient. In order to be truly obedient, we must be patient. Patience is faithfully waiting on the Lord, regardless of how long it may take.

A danger to becoming impatient is the desire for isolation. We can be drawn into isolating from one another because of past hurt, lack of trust, fear of vulnerability, and many other excuses. We need to wait together. We were made to be social beings. Finding a circle of trusted friends who are like-minded will have a tremendous impact on your overall well-being. These friends are people who will give you encouragement, love (sometimes tough), reprieve, joy, laughter, camaraderie, and compassion. They're people you can turn to for honest advice in difficult situations, people you can lean on when life is hard, and people you can be vulnerable with because you trust one another deeply.

We are far more likely to change when there are others in our life we want to change for. My wife and children were the ones whom I first began to change for, and they're still my biggest reason to continue changing for the better. However, we've been more open to God's call in our lives and have been intentional about our relationships outside of our home. We've developed deeper relationships with people that mean a great deal to us. Some of these relationships happened naturally, while others took a little more intentionality. They're each great in their own ways.

We also need to be available. Friendship isn't about what you can get from another person. It's about being available for someone else and sharing your wins and losses, praises and setbacks, and hopes and fears. It's a relationship that expresses love in a selfless, mutually uplifting way. If nothing else, it's simply about being *together*. Back to the isolation issue: when we face trials, many of us tend to isolate to deal with the problem alone. The stigma says having an issue is weakness and an embarrassment. We don't want to share that.

Here's a story from a personal experience on the receiving end of available friends:

My wife and I, along with many local volunteers, friends, professionals, and philanthropists, have worked over the last two years to open a nonprofit childcare facility in our community as the need for affordable, quality childcare in our area is extremely high. About a year and a half into the project, the time, money, and stress had taken its toll on Brittani. She was exhausted, emotionally drained, and overwhelmed by the negative cash flow, added workload, and large debt we had incurred to get the facility opened.

I did my best to comfort her and remind her that God had called us to take on this project, that He had brought us this far and no matter the circumstance, we can glorify Him through obedience to His calling.

I couldn't get through to her this time. It wasn't that she didn't believe what I was saying; it was that she felt like we were alone and might lose what we've worked so hard for: our house, our retirement, our reputations—all materialistic and superficial compared to God's glory. She knew she shouldn't worry, but her feelings were very real, and nothing I could say would change that.

So I texted two of her closest friends who are faithful, Godly women and briefly explained what was going on and asked that they pray for Brittani. It was vulnerable and uncomfortable because the situation felt so deeply private, but I trusted them.

The next morning at 6:00 am, available friend in our kitchen, we prayed together. It wasn't an immediate reversal in Brittani's mindset, but the load on her shoulders had significantly lightened, and within a few days, she was pretty much herself again. These wise, Godly women taught me two very valuable lessons that morning:

1. The power of availability
2. The power of presence

For where two or three gather in my name, there am I with them. (Matthew 18:20 NIV)

On our journey of faith, we need to be focused:
    Focused on the Father.
    Focused on our mindset.
    Focused on our goals.

On our journey of faith, we need to be prepared:
Prepared in the Word.
Prepared for His calling.
Prepared for the challenges we will ultimately face.

On our journey of faith, we need to be bold:
Bold in asking for what we need.
Bold in our relationships.
Bold in our outreach.

For most of us, spiritual growth will undoubtedly require change. Change will always require us to step out of our comfort zone. Growth in any worthwhile endeavor will be uncomfortable and maybe involve some pain. When it comes to your relationship with Jesus, no obstacle is too great it's not worth crossing.

Playing The Game

Sometimes the game is scary. Occasionally, we will strike out. In my last at-bat of my competitive baseball career, I went down swinging. I've thought about that moment a lot and what could have been. But you know what I finally realized? I went down *swinging*, not looking.

Winning this game isn't about anyone else. It's about you. It's about learning and growing. It's about finding your identity in Jesus Christ and His gift of forgiveness.

In life, it's important to know the playbook. But what's more important is actually playing. We learn through experiences, trials and errors, and failures and successes. Maybe life is just a game. But you get to have a say in the direction the game plays out. When it comes to being successful at this game, develop widsom. Wisdom isn't knowledge only. Wisdom is the reliability of action regarding the application of knowledge and experience. In other words: learn, then *do*. Be wise.

Go play.

Printed in the USA
CPSIA information can be obtained
at www.ICGtesting.com
LVHW062106180823
755631LV00007B/137